The Furman Singers

The Furman Singers

Discipline, Beauty, Excellence

♦ ♦ ♦

Dr. Troy David Robertson

Team Fields Publishing

Copyright © 2011 Dr. Troy David Robertson

2017 Revision – 2nd Edition

All Rights Reserved

No part of this publication may be reproduced, stored in a retrieval system, or transmitted in any form or by any means - electronic, mechanical, photocopy, recording or otherwise - without prior written permission.

ISBN: 098843623X
ISBN-13: 9780988436237
Cover Design: Kenneth E. Fields and Troy D. Robertson
Cover Photograph: *The Paladin* (furmannewspaper.com)
Editing: Sarah Bell and Kenneth E. Fields

I dedicate this effort to Stephanie Robertson, whose support has sustained me, and whose example has inspired me.

ACKNOWLEDGMENTS

Since completing the first version of this document in 2011, I have recounted often what a pleasure it was to produce. Spending time on campus, talking to dear friends old and new, and delving deep into the treasure troves of Furman Archives, Dave's Place, and Dr. Vick's file cabinets were experiences I would happily repeat. I was thrilled when Kenneth Fields ('98) approached me to turn it into a book available for all of Singers. Many thanks are due to Kenneth for starting that process, and to Sarah Bell ('77) for her help along the way.

I would also like to thank Dr. Bingham Vick, Jr. for all of his help. His tireless dedication to Furman Singers has been evident in my perusal of the many thousands of documents in the Furman Singers Archives and in many hours of conversation. Special thanks are due to Julia A. Cowert of Furman University Special Collections and Archives for her assistance, as well as her colleague DebbieLee Landi. My thanks go to Dr. Hugh Floyd, current director of Furman Singers, and Dr. Mark E. Britt, Professor of Trombone, for assisting me with access to Furman Singers Archives. Thanks as well to Emily Sweezey, administrative assistant to Dr. Britt, for her help in making sure I had daily access to those materials.

I would like to thank the individuals who contributed interview material to this project: Carolyn Dennis, Dr. Gordon Herring, Sarah

Herring, Dr. Lloyd Linney, Dave Vassy, Dr. Bruce Schoonmaker, Dr. David Parker, Dr. Hugh Floyd, James E. Williams, III, and Dr. Bingham Vick, Jr. I would offer special thanks to my family members, Ryan, Sara, and Emery Glenn, who provided housing during my many visits to Furman University.

I want to thank my supporters at Florida State University, who were the members of my dissertation committee: Dr. Christopher Moore, Dr. Judy Bowers, Dr. André Thomas, and Dr. Kevin Fenton. Their guidance helped make the process an enjoyable one, and I am grateful to them for their expertise and mentoring during my time at Florida State University. I wish to thank Dr. Fenton in particular, whose support and friendship has meant more than he can know.

I would like to thank my immediate family: my parents, Dave and Marisa Robertson, as well as my brother Reid Robertson. Their lifelong support and love have urged me on through years of teaching and years of school.

Finally, I would like to thank my wife, Dr. Stephanie Robertson, to whom this effort is dedicated. She is a constant source of encouragement and love. Moreover, she is an industrious scholar, and her example has inspired me throughout the writing process.

TABLE OF CONTENTS

	Acknowledgments · vii
Chapter 1	Introduction ·1
Chapter 2	Furman University ·6
Chapter 3	Early Choral Activity at Furman University · · · · · · · · · · · ·20
Chapter 4	Dupre Directed Me: The Tenure of Dupre Rhame · · · · ·52
Chapter 5	I Sing for Bing: The Tenure of Bingham Vick, Jr. · · · · · · ·74
Chapter 6	Always Make Music: An Examination of the Tour Repertoire of Furman Singers ·132

Appendix A Interview Transcriptions · · · · · · · · · · · · ·139
Appendix B Bibliography ·205
Appendix C List of Figures ·227
Biographical Sketch ·231

CHAPTER 1

INTRODUCTION

Furman University is located in Greenville, South Carolina. Furman University's name and location changed several times as the institution underwent changes in size and focus in the nineteenth century. Earlier names and locations included Edgefield, South Carolina as the "Furman Academy and Theological Institution," Fairfield, South Carolina under the same name, and Greenville, South Carolina (the downtown, or "old campus") as "The Furman University."

"Furman Singers" refers the choral ensemble founded in 1946 and first conducted by Dupre Rhame.

Furman University has been located in Greenville, South Carolina since 1851; however, no attempt will be made to chronicle the history of Greenville.[1]

The early history of Furman University

In order to understand the beginnings of Furman Singers it is also necessary to understand the reasons for the absence of any significant musical activity during the first 75 years of Furman University's history. Furman University was founded in 1826 and named for Richard Furman, a South Carolinian, prominent Baptist minister and leader, and lifelong advocate for Baptist education. Initially called the Furman Academy and Theological Institution, Furman

University had two primary purposes: to provide a general education for students enrolled in the academy and to train young men enrolled in the theological school for Baptist ministry. First located in Edgefield, South Carolina in the remnants of the John M. Roberts Academy, Furman opened in 1827 with an enrollment of four students. The first two instructors quit relatively quickly and the school would have closed permanently if a member of the executive board of the Charleston Association, Jesse Hartwell, had not volunteered to move Furman University's operations into his home. Hartwell managed to run the school with the assistance of Samuel Furman, Richard Furman's son, but eventually resigned and the school again moved, this time to Fairfield, South Carolina.

In moving to the Fairfield location, Furman University included farming as part of its curriculum, a common educational strategy of the time. In this case the combination of academy and farm did not succeed, however, and gradually the farming component was abandoned with an eye toward increased enrollment. Literary studies ceased in 1840, but theological studies continued and enrollment slowly increased. Three instructors, James Clement Furman (another of Richard Furman's sons), James Sessions Mims, and Peter Cuttino Edwards, constituted the theology faculty. During their tenure, Furman University's reputation continued to improve and expand through the state and region. James C. Furman would become president and lead the university through the next several decades.

In the 1840s Furman's direction began to change. The Southern Baptist Convention pushed for a seminary as part of the university's offerings as well as a degree-granting institution. These ideas found voice in the 1849 convention resolution to move and expand the school. On June 16, 1850 the convention made the decision to move the Furman Theological Seminary to Greenville and change its name to The Furman University. The school officially dropped the article from its name and became Furman University in 1866.

Enrollment continued to climb during this period, reaching a peak around 2,000 students, and Furman University enjoyed a period of sustained success. A decade later, however, that picture changed dramatically with the beginning of the Civil War. Only 30 students enrolled in the fall of 1861 and, facing sharp drops in enrollment and the stresses of war, Furman University closed its doors.

At its reopening in 1866 Furman University's enrollment was 140. The costs of war were apparent, and not just in numbers: only four names appearing on the 1861 rolls also appeared in 1866. The next several years were difficult ones for the school, but James C. Furman continued to work to improve the university's financial situation until resigning as president in 1879. Charles Manly replaced him in 1881. Under Manly, Furman University underwent a series of improvements that would slowly give the school renewed energy and strength, including a curriculum overhaul, the creation of student dormitories, expansion of student organizations, and continued work to increase the school's endowment. Andrew Philip Montague replaced Manly in 1897 and served as president through the beginning of the century. Montague's presidency marked the end of a long period of struggle and the beginning of greater financial security and refinement of purpose for Furman University.

Early choral activity at Furman University and the founding of Furman Singers

It was during this time of growth in the quality of student life at Furman University that musical activities on campus began to gain a place of greater prominence and eventually become an integral part of the curriculum. Glee clubs formed on campus in 1898, and in the first edition of Furman's yearbook, the *Bonhomie* of 1901, students listed a music club and faculty choir as part of the university clubs.[2] Included in the listing were the names and voice parts of the participants. Meanwhile, at the Greenville Woman's College, where music was very much an integral part of the curriculum, the first glee clubs appear in the student yearbook in 1912. In 1917, Professor George Schaeffer, director of music at the Greenville Woman's College, became the first faculty director of the glee clubs at Furman. Schaeffer continued in this role until 1922 and during that time took the students to tour churches around Furman University, housing them in congregation members' homes at each stop. Glee clubs traveled farther afield in subsequent years, as some of Furman University's clubs found their way to performances in New York City during the 1920s.[3] Over the course of the next decade musical opportunities continued to grow both at Furman University and the Greenville Woman's College.

In 1934 Furman University and the Greenville Woman's College combined and, until the outbreak of World War II, the two student bodies mingled, attending classes on both campuses and collaborating in their musical ensembles. At the time of this integration DuPre Rhame directed Furman's glee club and assumed directorship of the music department. Rhame would go on to found Furman Singers in 1946, after the conclusion of World War II, when young men once again began to audition for singing ensembles on campus.

Soon after its founding, Furman Singers became a vital part of campus life and, over the next several decades, a vital part of cultural life in the surrounding area. Furman Singers toured and continues to tour each year, usually in the southeast. In its early years the ensemble made up the majority of the singing cast for Furman University's various student opera, operetta, and oratorio performances. This pattern continued until Rhame's retirement in the fall of 1970. At that time Furman University hired Bingham Vick, Jr. to take Rhame's place. Vick's first year included a national radio broadcast of Furman Singers' annual performance of George Frideric Handel's *Messiah* as well as a shift in direction toward art music of the choral tradition. The next year, Furman Singers performed at the national convention of the American Choral Directors Association (ACDA). Furman Singers' history since 1970 is marked by dozens of tours of various parts of the United States, 20 tours of Europe and Asia, a number of national and regional ACDA performances, performances of new works by composers such as Howard Hanson, and collaborations with other musical organizations including the Boston Pops. Vick retired in the spring of 2010 and Furman University hired Hugh Floyd, a Furman alumnus, to take Vick's place as director of Furman Singers.

In the words of John Tosh, the "historian's business is to construct interpretations of the past from its surviving remains."[4] The facts of the history of Furman Singers are not reflected in any detail in the three primary histories of Furman University. Most of the information related to the ensemble's history resides in scattered collections of documents in Furman University's Special Collections and Archives department of the James B. Duke Library, including scrapbooks lovingly crafted by students at the conclusion of each year. Some information may be found in periodicals such as Furman's student publications, periodicals, and newspapers such as the *Greenville News* that have, at one time or another, covered performances of Furman Singers. Other information related to this history resides only in the memories of former members of the ensemble. This narrative of the history of Furman Singers has been constructed by documenting and examining these disparate sources of information.

---

1 Former Furman professor and vice president Archie Vernon Huff, Jr.'s 1995 book, *Greenville: The History of the City and County in the South Carolina Piedmont*, provides a relatively recent and exhaustive look at Greenville's history.
2 The first editions of the *Bonhomie* through the year 1932 and the Greenville Woman's College course catalogues may be found at the following URL: <http://digicenter2.furman.edu/luna/servlet/furmanfdc~56~56?cic=furmanfdc%7E56%7E56>
3 David Parker. *Discipline, Perfection, and Beauty: A History of Choral Music at Furman University and Greenville Woman's College, 1900-1987.* (Columbia, South Carolina: University of South Carolina Press, 1995), 33.
4 John Tosh. *The Pursuit of History: Aims, Methods, and New Directions in the Study of Modern History.* (United Kingdom: Pearson Education Limited, 2006), 88.

CHAPTER 2

FURMAN UNIVERSITY

Baptist Beginnings

Until its separation from the Baptist denomination in 1991, Furman University was the oldest Baptist educational institution in the southern United States, and Furman University's founding traces to the very first Baptists in South Carolina.[1] These colonists were part of a growing denomination that needed ministers to guide its churches and congregations, and it was out of this need that the concept for a Baptist institution of learning grew. Alfred Sandlin Reid writes that Furman University, "like many colleges and universities founded between the American Revolution and the Civil War," also owes its origins, in part, to a growing sense of nationalism in the American colonies.[2]

The Baptist denomination found its first foothold in South Carolina in the city of Charleston with the founding of the Charleston Church in 1683.[3] These early Baptists faced harsh prejudice from their fellow colonists and, as a consequence, grew slowly in number. Meanwhile, in the northeastern colonies, Baptists flourished, and prominent among them was George Whitefield. One of the men influenced by Whitefield's preaching was Oliver Hart.[4] Oliver Hart was a Pennsylvania Quaker, but he became inspired by Whitefield and decided to become a Baptist minister in 1746, sailing to South Carolina in 1749 to answer the colony's need for ministers.[5]

During the 1740s South Carolina Baptists had only one active minister, Isaac Chanler. Oliver Hart arrived shortly after Chanler's death in 1749, and Hart assumed the position of pastor at Charleston Church on February 16, 1750. His new parishioners viewed his arrival as providential.[6] During the next year Hart set about the work of providing ministry to the city of Charleston and organized the four churches in the area into the Charleston Association. Opportunities for formal study were few at that time. Rhode Island College (now Brown University) was founded in 1765 and was the first Baptist college in the colonies. Rhode Island College, while a great distance away, attracted the "support and attention" of the Charleston Association, whose interest in education continued to grow until the outbreak of the Revolutionary War.[7] The Baptists' role in the colonies' attempt to break with England forced Oliver Hart to flee Charleston to the Euhaw tribe's lands on October 6, 1775.[8]

After the tumultuous Revolutionary War years, Richard Furman became the leader of the Baptists in South Carolina and replaced Oliver Hart at Charleston Church. Richard Furman was born in Esopus, New York on October 9, 1755.[9] His parents were Wood and Rachel Furman, farmers who moved to South Carolina shortly after Richard Furman's birth. It seems likely that this move was made in response to the royal governor of South Carolina's offer of land grants in an effort to push back the frontier. Wood Furman moved several times during his son's childhood, and his final move did not take place until 1770 when he relocated his family to the High Hills of Santee.

Richard Furman's education was largely informal, though thorough. He was a child of enormous aptitude and showed great interest in the Bible from a very early age. In May of 1774, at the age of 18, Furman was ordained and became the pastor of the Baptist church at High Hills. Later that year Oliver Hart came to visit the church at High Hills to learn more of the "Separates."[10] Furman had married Elizabeth Haynsworth in November, and his ministry was well underway. Furman's friendship with Hart began with that visit. Shortly thereafter the two of them became active with the revolutionary cause and Hart was forced to flee South Carolina.

Furman's relationship with the Revolutionary War was not official or martial, but he preached on the subject and a good part of his subsequent reputation rested on his involvement in the revolution.[11] His efforts attracted the attention of the British, as well, and Lord Cornwallis placed a price on Furman's head. The young preacher eventually fled the state, returning in 1782, after the war's conclusion.[12] On his return, he continued to serve the High Hills church until 1787, when he became the minister to the Charleston Church.

Furman's ties to Charleston did not begin with his move to the Charleston Church. In 1779 the Charleston Association found that it needed an executive board to carry out administrative functions, and appointed Evan Pugh, Edmund Botsford, Richard Furman, and John Cowan to a committee that served as a liaison for the Charleston Association, recommended new ministers, screened existing ministers, and performed other duties as deemed necessary. In 1786, Furman was elected moderator of the Charleston Association, and he used that platform to further his interest in education for young, aspiring ministers. This effort took the form of the Charleston Baptist Education Fund, created in 1792 under the auspices of the Charleston Association. Over the years this fund assisted with the education of many prominent Baptists, including Jesse Mercer, founder of Mercer University.[13]

Richard Furman conceived of education as something of practical value, especially to ministers, and described his conception of the usefulness of the Charleston Baptist Education Fund in such terms: "The education, or improvement, contemplated in the query, does not consist in a gingle, or pomp of words; in idle speculations; trifling criticisms; or a vain philosophy: but in solid, rational, and useful knowledge."[14] He pressed for better education for Baptist ministers throughout his career, and in 1790, the Charleston Association appointed Furman, Silas Mercer, Benjamin Mosely, and Henry Holcombe to a committee whose task was to develop a plan for creating a more permanent solution to aiding aspiring Baptist ministers in South Carolina.[15] This committee came to be known as the "General Committee" and held its first meeting with the Charleston Association in 1791. At that time the only plan for education was the adoption of prospective ministers by established ministers. The young men lived with their mentors' families and utilized the elder ministers' books for study. The advent of the Roberts Academy marked the first change from this model.

In 1800 the Charleston Association adopted the academy at High Hills Baptist Church as the "chief agency for the education of beneficiaries of the general committee."[16] This academy, later known as the Roberts Academy after its director, John M. Roberts, represented the first educational institution under the auspices of the Baptists of South Carolina. The Roberts Academy benefited from the support of the Charleston Association in the purchase of a theological library. This library would become the foundation of the Furman Theological Institute's library. The Roberts Academy was short-lived, however, and William Joseph McGlothlin infers from the minutes of the Charleston Association that the Roberts Academy was defunct by 1810. For the 15 years intervening between the closing of the academy and the opening of the Furman Theological Institute, South Carolina Baptists again had no school for the training of ministers.[17]

Richard Furman's influence within the Baptist denomination continued to grow during these years. He was elected president of the American Baptists at the first general meeting of the Baptists in Philadelphia in 1814. He was reelected in 1817. In that capacity he led the way to the creation of a national Baptist institution in

Washington D.C., all the while stressing the need for religious education. He also led in organizing the South Carolina Baptist Convention, and, in the adoption of a constitution, its delegates emphasized the importance of education based on "principles of Christian liberality, and in favor of the rights of private judgment." Richard Furman died in August of 1825, but his continued push for a material commitment to education on the part of the Baptists would, late in that same year, lead to a major shift in the focus of aid to ministers, away from simple mentoring and toward the creation of a new institution.

Furman University's First 75 Years

The South Carolina Baptist Convention incorporated on December 20, 1825, so that it could own property. The time had come to create its own educational institution. Initial plans called for a school to be located at Edgefield, South Carolina. The following year, 1826, is the year shown on Furman University's seal as the year of the university's founding, and several important events occurred in that year.

At a meeting in Edgefield on March 16 and 17, a quorum of the Board of Agents, six people in total, met to accept the properties of the Village Academy, a school in the area donated by the trustees of that institution. Months later, in September, the Board of Agents approved Joseph Andrew Warne as the first principal of the new academy. The South Carolina Baptist Convention approved Warne's appointment in November and, on December 19, agreed to name the academy the Furman Academy and Theological Institution in honor of Richard Furman.[18] The school would be owned and directed by the convention, the daily business to be conducted by an executive committee comprised of the Board of Agents living in the Edgefield area. Professors were to be comprised of Baptists or individuals amenable to the Baptist denomination. Admission to the academy was open to "any youth, whose education shall be paid for, without regard to sect or denomination."[19]

On January 15, 1827, the Furman Academy and Theological Institution opened for its first day of exercises. Only a few students attended that first quarter, and the hope and promise of the South Carolina Baptist Convention's initial action was dampened by lack of support from Georgia Baptists or the local Edgefield Association. The school's enrollment would remain low throughout its first 25 years of existence, at around ten students each quarter. Warne suffered from poor health and did not remain at the school long, tendering his resignation in June of 1828. The South Carolina Baptist Convention met in December of 1828 and, in light of the lack of funding and suitable personnel to ensure its continued operation, resolved that the classical department, the non-theological component of the school, close and the ministerial students relocate. Ministerial students continued to study with the Reverend Jesse Hartwell at his private home in the High Hills.

Hartwell's tutelage was intended to be a temporary solution, but the executive board relied heavily on Hartwell's labors for five years. The 35-year-old minister constructed crude housing for his students at his own expense, students who first numbered only a few, but by April, 1830, numbered 12. Observing Hartwell's struggles, the executive board approved an assistant, hiring Samuel Furman, one of Richard Furman's sons, to teach alongside Hartwell. This relationship was not to be a happy one, and this strain contributed to the arrangement's brief duration. In that same year James C. Furman, another son of Richard Furman and a man who would later become president of the institution, matriculated at the High Hills.

Four years later, however, the school was once again in crisis, as both Hartwell and Samuel Furman resigned. It would remain closed for the next three years, but in 1835 the executive board moved toward reopening the school and appointed a Board of Trustees to oversee its operations. This was done in the hope that a smaller committee with greater authority might better manage the difficulties associated with operating the school through the South Carolina Baptist Convention. At this time, under the influence of the upper part of the state, manual labor became compulsory for students in the English and classical department of the school. This experiment in farming alongside education accounted, in part, for the executive board's decision to move the school from High Hills to Fairfield. The land at High Hills was not especially fertile, and, utilizing money from the sale of the land and buildings there, the board purchased land near Winnsboro, South Carolina's Fairfield Church.

Closing briefly for the move, the classical academy of the Furman Academy and Theological Institution opened in the Fairfield district under the direction of W.E. Bailey in 1837. The theology department reopened a year later under William Hooper. Before the school's proceedings were well underway, however, a fire marred the joy of a fresh start. The Fairfield location's building used for housing the students, classrooms, and library was 120 feet in length and 30 to 40 feet in width. This frame building burned on May 1, 1837. The blaze killed one of the students, Francis Goddard, and completely destroyed the school's holdings. Local neighbors of the school took the students into their homes and Bailey insisted that classes continue. Between May of that year and January of 1838 new buildings were constructed and attendance resumed its climb. Farming continued as part of the curriculum, but students did not prove amenable to the idea of manual labor, and discipline problems increased. At the end of 1839 the executive board moved to end the manual labor portion of students' English studies. Though theology studies continued, literary studies ceased shortly after the end of the farming initiative in 1840. Theology instructors had been in a state of flux, but three individuals finally provided a stable faculty: James Clement Furman, James Session Mims, and Peter Cuttino

Edwards. During these three men's tenure, the school's reputation began to improve and expand.

Furman's decades of labor on behalf of the school would be marked by hardship. This eventuality was not unanticipated even as Furman accepted his appointment. His sister wrote the following on receiving the news that Furman was leaving the ministry to teach at the small school:

> We all heard with regret for your own sakes the removal from Society Hill. We feared the change on many accounts would not be desirable, and that your health would suffer from the constant mental effort, which your new duties would render necessary…You have relinquished much in entering upon your new station and I hope that you may be rewarded for doing so, by having your labours crowned with success.[20]

Despite these various hardships, James C. Furman proved to be an untiring and intensely loyal partisan for the school throughout his long tenure.

Furman led the faculty in a reorganization of the theological school into four departments in 1844: Biblical Literature and Interpretation, Biblical Theology, Sacred Rhetoric and Pastoral Duties, and Ecclesiastical History. The new structure and prosperity seemed to bode well for the Fairfield venture, but the South Carolina Baptist Convention as well as the theological school's faculty desired more for South Carolina: all parties agreed that a cooperative seminary, a degree-granting institution, could do more to advance the education of young ministers than the humble school had done thus far. James C. Furman expressed his views in a letter to William Jenkins, a letter whose tone presages Furman's support for South Carolina's secession: "The time has come when we can no longer send to the North, and if our brethren will only endow our institution we shall have a place for our young brethren preparing for the ministry to which they can resort without going to the North."[21]

The South Carolina Baptist Convention's desire to expand the scope of the institution necessitated yet another move, this time to a more populous area. The northwestern part of the state seemed an attractive option, described in another letter by Furman, who was charged with chairing the committee seeking a new location for the school:

> In view of this change in the mode of operation of the Institution many members thought it highly important to place the Institution at a point where it might enjoy the advantages of denser white population and greater facility of railroad communication. Greenville and Anderson, the two termini of the Columbia and Greenville Railroad and Greenwood in Abbeville, which is upon the line of the same road, were spoken of as places, either of which would afford these advantages, and where an enlightened public sentiment and strong denominational sympathy would ensure for the Institution a desirable location.[22]

The committee would decide in favor of Greenville on June 16, 1850, and on December 20, 1850 obtained the charter of "The Furman University."

The 1840s and 1850s were a prosperous time for the town of Greenville, and the population grew steadily from 1,100 in 1843 to 1,750 in 1852. Greenville's merchants were few, comprising just 3.9 percent of the population, and the surrounding county based its economy on farming cotton, corn, and grain. Though the Civil War loomed ahead, the new location and final decade of the antebellum period made for a time of growth for The Furman University, which opened again in early 1851, before any buildings had been constructed. The university gained two schools in addition to the theology department: a college preparatory department and a college. The executive board also planned to add schools of law and medicine. James C. Furman spent the first year of operations fundraising, while James Session Mims took charge of the seminary and Edwards took the academy. Charles Hallette Judson joined the faculty in November of that year.

As The Furman University underwent its move, the South Carolina Baptist Convention considered the role of education for females at a level approximately commensurate with the collegiate-level education offered the new university at Greenville. These considerations came to fruition on July 25, 1854 with the adoption of the resolution to establish the "Greenville Baptist Female College." This school would, through its connections with the South Carolina Baptist Convention, remain closely tied to The Furman University, eventually integrating with it in the next century.

In 1852 The Furman University opened the first of its new buildings, McBee Hall with a total enrollment of 68 students. The school now granted three degrees: Proficient, Bachelor's, and Master's. Over the next eight years The Furman University enjoyed unprecedented growth and expansion, including the construction of new buildings and the iconic Florentine bell tower.[23] Discussions in the South Carolina Baptist Convention begun in the early 1840s would once again lead to a splintering of the university's purpose, however.

Though South Carolina now had its own seminary in The Furman University, Georgia, Alabama, and North Carolina all were interested in a central seminary for Baptists in the South. The South Carolina Baptists were in agreement with the neighboring states, and discussion centered on beginning a new cooperative seminary at The Furman University location with $30,000 of the university's endowment, its theological faculty, and its theological library. This effort was led, in part, by James Petigru Boyce, who replaced James Mims after Mims' death in 1855. Boyce was, like James C. Furman, a student of the College of Charleston, Madison (now Colgate), Brown, and Princeton. In the fall of 1859 the seminary opened with 26 students, functioning as a separate entity from The Furman University.

Figure 2.1 – The Florentine Bell Tower and surrounding campus, "Old Campus" location. Photo courtesy Furman University Special Collections and Archives.

As the Baptists discussed the fate of their new seminary, the conflict between Unionists and Secessionists raged in Greenville throughout the 1850s. Matters came to a head in the summer of 1860, and James C. Furman was in the midst of it. He was elected chair of a public meeting on May 21 held to discuss the southern states' options with regard to the maintenance of slavery and protection of their interests. Later that year, in the Secession Convention held in December, James C. Furman traveled to Columbia to represent the Greenville district as a South Carolinian and a slaveholder, an owner of forty-one slaves.[24] The Ordinance of Secession was approved by unanimous consent on December 20.

Following the signing of the ordinance, The Furman University's students began to enlist in the mustering armies. So many enlisted, in fact, that commencement exercises for the spring were canceled. In the fall of 1861, facing an enrollment of only 30 and no students in its halls, The Furman University once again was forced to close its doors. Professors Furman and Judson continued to teach at the Female College during the war years, while Edwards continued to work at the university, managing a high school under his own auspices. Under Charles Judson's presidency, the college, though struggling, remained open through the war and afterwards.

In 1866, with an enrollment of 140 students and now called Furman University, the school reopened at the initiative of the faculty, not the South Carolina Baptist Convention. This glimmer of hope proved short-lived, however, as enrollment declined immediately, and the school closed once again in 1868. James C. Furman continued to push for the university's interests, even in the face of the many financial obstacles facing the university in the wake of the Civil War: "I have been urged to abandon the university and seek a field of labor more certain. But I have resolved, if the university should go down, to sink with it."[25]

Furman faced more problems than Reconstruction, however, and though the partnership with the Southern Baptist Theological Seminary offered early promise, decreased demand for the college, independent of demand for the seminary, kept the university's growth stagnant for many years. The refusal to require collegiate education as a prerequisite for entry to the seminary enhanced this stagnation. In 1877, with backing from the convention, the seminary relocated to its current home in Louisville, Kentucky. In 1879, following this move, Furman University's faculty temporarily resigned and the trustees of the university suspended operations until 1881.

Sadly, this dire period in the university's history marked the end of James C. Furman's tenure as president. Furman resigned along with the rest of the faculty in 1879, though he would continue to teach at the school until his death in 1891, having given 50 years of his life to the institution.

The executive board called Charles Manly to replace Furman as president in 1881. Manly would remain in that office until 1897, overseeing the university's long recovery. For the first few years of Manly's presidency enrollment remained static at around 100 students. In financial terms, Furman University's position did not become more secure until 1890, when Manly succeeded in raising the much-needed sum of $20,000 to garner an offer of $7,500 from the American Baptist Education Society, bringing the total endowment to $75,500. Curriculum and student life also improved under Manly: he undertook a curriculum overhaul and initiated the construction of "messes" or dormitories to assist students hoping to avoid the high cost of living in private homes. Students also began to establish social, religious, and athletic organizations. It was in 1892 that students began to publish the *Furman Echo,* a literary magazine still in publication today. On December 14, 1889, Furman University played Wofford in South Carolina's first intercollegiate football game. In 1893 the trustees of the university voted to make the school coeducational, an effort they reversed in 1900, citing the small number of women students and the continued operation of the Greenville Woman's College, formerly the Female College.

President Manly resigned in 1897 in response to the trustees' insistence that he devote all of his time to the university rather than accepting preaching and pastoral assignments. Andrew Philip Montague, a professor of Latin from Columbia University, became

Manly's successor after unanimous approval by the trustees. Alfred Sandlin Reid calls Montague Furman University's "first lay scholar with administrative assistance," and Montague's presidency marked the beginning of the university's preparations to face the challenges of a new century of growth.

---

1 From the preface to William Joseph McGlothlin's Baptist Beginnings in Education: A History of Furman University. (Nashville, Tennessee: 1926).
2 Alfred Sandlin Reid. Furman University: Toward a New Identity. (Durham, North Carolina: Duke University Press, 1976), 3.
3 Joe M. King. A History of South Carolina Baptists. (Columbia, South Carolina: The R. L. Bryan Company, 1964), 10.
4 McGlothlin, 22.
5 King, 17.
6 McGlothlin, 24.
7 McGlothlin, 26.
8 King, 19.
9 King, 21.
10 King, 22.
11 Rogers, 28.
12 King, 23.
13 King, 23.
14 Richard Furman, quoted in Reid, 3-4.
15 King, 160-161.
16 McGlothlin, 35-36.
17 McGlothlin, 38.
18 Reid, 6.
19 The minutes of the South Carolina Baptist Convention, quoted in Reid, 6.
20 Harvey Tolliver Cook. The Life Work of James Clement Furman. (Greenville, South Carolina: 1926), 103.
21 James C. Furman quoted in Cook, The Life Work of James Clement Furman, 106.
22 James C. Furman quoted in Cook, The Life Work of James Clement Furman, 120.
23 Reid, 10.
24 Huff, 134.
25 Huff, 201.

CHAPTER 3

EARLY CHORAL ACTIVITY AT FURMAN UNIVERSITY

Furman University's Choral Activities in Context

At the beginning of the 20th century, the administration of Furman University afforded students more opportunities in social settings, more license in the formation of academic and social clubs, and athletics featured far more prominently on campus. Alfred Sandlin Reid cites 1898 as the year in which students formed the first Furman Glee Club.[1] In 1934, a *Furman Hornet* article detailing the club's plans for tour gives some details of the club's founding in its final paragraph: "The present year marks the thirty-sixth season of the musicians as an organization, the club having been founded in 1898 by the late Professor George A. Buist."[2] The first extant, contemporaneous university record of an ensemble resembling a glee club, however, dates from the 1900 to 1901 school year and the first volume of the *Bonhomie*, Furman University's student yearbook.[3]

The formation of Furman University's glee clubs was part of a larger, national trend. J. Perry White and George N. Heller, in their article, "Entertainment, Enlightenment, and Service: A History and Description of Choral Music in Higher Education," attempted to create a taxonomy for choral ensembles past and present.[4] They identified three trends in the nation's colleges and universities. All three trends were present at Furman University. The first of these trends, the "Gleeful Choir," dominated choral activity at Furman University until the 1930s. The name of these early ensembles, "glee," comes from a mid-17th century word for an entertainment. Tracing its history to the medieval "catch," by the middle of the 18th century, "glee" referred to a part song, especially part songs for unaccompanied men's voices.[5] The form was largely an English phenomenon, and it was as part of this tradition that clubs in the United States took shape.

The first American university glee club began at Harvard in 1858, and glee clubs became very popular on college and university campuses by the turn of the 20th century. Typical repertoire included sacred and secular selections, so-called "novelty" songs, and school songs. In this, the Furman Glee Club fit the norm. Judging by the repertoire of glee clubs and the playfulness with which their membership constructed concert programs, their popularity was driven in large part by student enjoyment and student agency.

Figure 3.1 – An early picture of members of the Furman Glee Club. Photo courtesy Furman University Special Collections and Archives.

The second trend identified by White and Heller, the "Chorale Esoterica," or chorus centered on challenging (and, in White and

Heller's view, elitist) repertoire, became part of choral activity during the latter part of the 1920s. This set of repertoire held a more prominent position in the activity of DuPre Rhame's tenure. The third trend, the "Public Service Choir," was part of the glee club experience from its inception. White and Heller define this last branch of activity as the performance of repertoire that benefits the society around the university as much as the students themselves, repertoire to accompany ceremonies and entertain audiences rather than educate or challenge students. They give as example arrangements of popular music and contemporary sacred literature intended for events such as graduation ceremonies.

Though White and Heller's terminology did not take hold, the "Gleeful Choir" is still termed "Glee Club," and the "Public Service Choir" is a component of many singing ensembles' activity. The "Chorale Esoterica" of their formulation is best known as part of the "A Cappella Choir" tradition. This tradition began with the touring choirs of the late 1890s and early 1900s. An early example, Frank Damrosch's Musical Art Society was an entirely professional ensemble of 50 voices. Other ensembles performing and touring at the time included the Mendelssohn Choir of Toronto, under the direction of A.S. Vogt, and the Schola Cantorum of New York, conducted by Kurt Schindler. All three choirs, through their tours of the United States, served as models for choral conductors seeking ways to improve their art. The successors to these choirs were the first collegiate a cappella ensembles. The Northwestern University A Cappella Choir, directed by Peter Christian Lutkin, the St. Olaf Lutheran Choir, led by F. Melius Christiansen, and the Westminster Choir, conducted by John Finley Williamson formed and toured in the wake of the Musical Art Society.

During the early period of these groups' popularity, at the outbreak of World War I, United States government officials saw choral singing as a means of improving citizens' morale. Through the formation of "Liberty Choruses," community choruses organized by councils of defense, participation and interest in choruses and choral music increased throughout the nation, adding to the appeal of a cappella singing for audiences. The influence of the "A Cappella" movement on campus life became apparent as, in the late 1920s, especially in the midst of the Great Depression, formation of mixed choirs increased sharply at co-educational institutions. These choirs' emphasis was on shorter, unaccompanied works. Later, in the 1930s, Fred Waring organized a small, professional men's glee club as part of his musical offerings with his band "Fred Waring's Pennsylvanians." Waring hired a young Robert Shaw to prepare the ensemble, and Shaw would in turn become one of the greatest influences on choral music in the 20th century. Shaw also formed his own chorale, as did his contemporary Roger Wagner. Together these ensembles helped shape college conductors' sense of direction with regard to repertoire and best practices. Over approximately 50 years, paralleling these developments, Furman University's glee clubs formed and evolved into Furman Singers.

The Furman University and Greenville Woman's College Glee Clubs

Furman University's *Bonhomie* is its annual yearbook. The first volume was published in 1901 with the first university record of a singing ensemble. Several ensembles are pictured, in fact, and the first to be pictured is "Ye Faculty Choir," a double quartet of eight singers. Under the heading "Object," the student editors wrote "Good Music at Chapel." An organist and stage master are listed in addition to "Ye Sopranos and Top-lines," "Ye Tenors," "Ye First Basses," and "Ye Second Basses." Clearly the students intended the archaically formal pronouns, combined with the following criticism, to poke fun at the faculty: "Critics…Student body. Criticism: Every one of our dear professors graduated at the Boston Conservatory of Music, for we cannot appreciate the delicate, complex harmony." Appearing a few pages past the faculty choir, the student ensemble, more humbly entitled "The Screechers," was made up of 14 singers and boasted a high degree of student-led organization, including a president, vice president, musical director, and vocal director.

Figure 3.2 – The Furman Glee Club of 1903. Photo courtesy Furman University Special Collections and Archives.

The 1902 and 1903 *Bonhomie* depict singing clubs of similar size and makeup, including an ensemble titled "Glee Club." Singing appears to have been a popular pastime not limited to the glee club setting; the formation of glee clubs was an outgrowth of an activity the students enjoyed in their mess halls and around the campus. As evidence of this, the *Bonhomie* includes pictures of various quartets and trios of young men throughout these early years of publication. Among the more unusual examples of these small groups was the "Bill Quartet" of 1913, comprised of Bill P. Carson, Bill V. Zeigler, Bill P. Sawyer, and E. Bill Machen. Another ensemble was listed simply as "Quartette," two tenors and two basses, in connection with the Glee Club.

Furman University's "Alma Mater" was among the songs important to the Glee Club. In 1909, Edwin M. Poteat's verses made their first appearance in the *Bonhomie*:

> The Mountain City is her home.
> A mountain river laves her feet,
> But from far coasts her children come,
> And crown her brow with flowers sweet;
> And 'neath her shade they rest secure,
> And drink from wisdom's fountain pure,
> And rally, loyal sons and true,
> 'Round our dear Alma Mater.
>
> A ship of loyal make is she,
> And brings her treasure from afar.
> Her truth it is that makes us free
> And shines her beacon like a star.
> 'Twas Furman's hand that laid her keel,
> And Judson set her ribs of steel;
> The Fathers, prayerful for our weal,
> Launched our dear Alma Mater.
>
> A mother gentle, fair, and wise,
> And grave with weight of storied lore,
> She greets us with love's radiant eyes
> And chains our hearts forevermore.
> Old Furman! grateful sons are we,
> Our love, our lives we give to thee;
> We'll keep faith's vow to serve but thee,
> Our own dear Alma Mater.[6]

The tune indicated for performance is Haydn's "Creation," the melody actually originating from a chorus in *The Creation*, "The Heavens Are Telling." The verses' origin lies in a contest held by the Furman University faculty to craft an alma mater in the spring of 1907. Poteat was president of the school at the time and won the contest. He might have been suspected of unfairly influencing the judgment of the faculty had he not been the sole entrant. Professor H.W.B. Barnes, head of the music department at the Greenville Woman's College, arranged Haydn's tune for use with the verses, and some years later composed an original melody, which has become the traditional strain.[7]

The first mention of a glee club at the Greenville Woman's College, which was called the Greenville Female College until the summer of 1914, occurs in the *Entre Nous* of 1912, the yearbook for the Greenville Woman's College. Though this ensemble appears nearly two decades later than ensembles of similar type at Furman University, music played a larger role in campus life and academic studies at the Greenville Woman's College. In its dual role as both an academic institution and a kind of finishing school, the college's "Special Studies," or what might be termed elective courses, emphasized music above all else. The music department enjoyed the largest enrollment of any academic division, the greatest number of faculty, and the greatest selection of course offerings.

The earliest extant printed music program in the Furman University Special Collections and Archives dates from 1914. It presents a joint concert by the Furman University Glee Club and the Greenville Female College. The personnel for the concert included an 18-piece orchestra of strings, a few wind players and brass, and two percussionists, the first orchestra of its size listed by the *Bonhomie*. The concert's repertoire varied widely from one selection to the next in terms of character and forces. For example, Abt's "Barcarole," performed by the combined clubs, opened the concert and was immediately followed by a cornet solo. Among the other selections on the concert were "My Wild Irish Rose" sung by the Furman University Quartette, the "Lustspiel Overture" by Kella Bella performed by the orchestra, and an unspecified solo performed by a member of the Furman University Glee Club. Non-musical performances were an important part of glee club appearances, and this concert featured an unspecified reading by a member of the Greenville Female College Glee Club.

Though the program lists no director nor does the *Bonhomie*, it is likely that the Furman University Glee Club, like its Greenville Female College counterpart, had a faculty director. Professor C.E. Poston directed the Furman University Glee Club in the 1915-1916 school year. George H. Schaefer replaced Poston in the fall of 1916 and remained director until 1922. It was under Schaefer's direction that the tradition of touring local schools and churches in the early spring began.

Figure 3.3 – A flyer for a Greenville Woman's College Glee Club concert, undated. Photo courtesy Furman University Special Collections and Archives.

Part of the draw of performance in the Furman University Glee Club was the opportunity to visit the young women at the Greenville Woman's College and elsewhere. Browsing descriptions of Glee Club activity in the *Furman Hornet*, Furman University's student paper from 1916 through 1961, quickly reveals this theme, and it seems likely that participation in the Greenville Woman's College Glee Club was motivated by similar impulses. Other students in the surrounding area visited each school, as well. In a description of an Anderson College Glee Club visit, a school that was at that time female-only, a *Furman Hornet* editor wrote the following:

> The program consisted of club numbers, quartets, piano solos, vocal solos, Scotch dances, and specialties...In the late afternoon prior to the concert, the Furman Glee Club had the pleasure of entertaining the visiting club...maybe it was the punch that made the young ladies sing so well in the concert! – and it wasn't "spiked" either.[8]

Below the description is printed a letter from the women of the Anderson College:

> Since we have returned and told all the girls about our trip, we have all decided that the Furman boys are the best ever, and they all appreciate as much as we do everything that you did to make our stay with you memorable. We want you all to know that you are welcome in Anderson. Come to see us when you can.

Though tragic in its consequences, World War I did far less than World War II to interrupt these idyllic interactions between the male and female campuses. The Great War did have an effect, however, and Volume 19 of the *Bonhomie* includes a page dedicated to the Furman University students who fought as soldiers in World War I and gives the students' impression of events:

> Even before America severed diplomatic relationships with Germany, there were those who gave themselves in this great cause, entering French and British units as soldiers, ambulance drivers, and surgeons. By May, 1917, so many undergraduates had volunteered that the student ranks were visibly depleted, and several Seniors came from nearby camps to receive their diplomas. The number grew continually until more than 320 men of the Purple and White were in service.⁹

Figure 3.4 – Furman students in field exercises, preparing for duty in World War I. The bell tower and old campus are in the background. Photo courtesy Furman University Special Collections and Archives.

The 1920s was a decade of continued growth for Furman University and success for the Glee Club. In the spring of 1921, DuPre Rhame, who would eventually become the first director of

Furman Singers, matriculated at Furman University. A native of Sumter, South Carolina, Rhame first entered Davidson College near Charlotte, North Carolina where he attended classes and played football, but transferred to Furman to participate in the school's music program. He may not have been able to participate in the Glee Club in the spring, however, though the 1921 *Bonhomie* does not list him among the personnel for that year, the *Bonhomie* of 1924 lists him as a four-year participant in the club. The 1921 volume also indicates that he took an immediate role in the university's athletics, playing football and managing the freshman basketball team.

Figure 3.5 – DuPre Rhame as a senior at Furman University. Photo courtesy Furman University Special Collections and Archives.

The 1924 *Bonhomie* lists Rhame's many activities while a student at Furman University, including participation in the Adelphian Literary Society, football, basketball, managing circulation for the *The Furman Hornet*, editing the "Clubs" section of the *Bonhomie*, student government, band, and orchestra. It also provides a brief idea of the high esteem in which he was held by his peers:

> "The noblest Roman of them all," we can rarely think of Furman without immediately calling to mind this son of Sumter. Truly he is the epitome of all the lofty ideals and purposes by which the Furman spirit is ever characterized. No pen could do fitting justice to him and his unswerving loyalty to his college and his class. "Pre's" achievements are legion and his has been the guiding spirit in numerous organizations which make up student life on the hill. His scholarship is as eminent as his friends are numerous, and his frankness and cordial friendliness have won for him the greatest esteem. We predict for him a future of marvelous brilliancy.[10]

By his sophomore year, Rhame had become an invaluable part of the Glee Club as a singer and as an instrumentalist, as instruments played a large role in the Glee Club's tour program. His contributions to the richly varied repertoire of 1922 included a xylophone solo:

> Either the Purple Stringers, the Junior Six, or the Carolina Roamers [instrumental ensembles comprised of students at Furman University] will accompany the Club. These musical organizations are famed for the sweetness of their music,

and any one of them will prove a pleasing addition to the program. Mr. DuPre Rhame will delight his hearers with charming music from a $250 xylophone.[11]

Rhame would perform xylophone solos on programs throughout his career as an undergraduate at Furman University. Under the direction of George Schaefer, the Glee Club's performances also continued to be evenings of general entertainment, rather than exclusively focused on the club's music:

> In addition to the Club and the musical organization, the presence of two comedians of note will make the program even more attractive. "Red" Burdette, who accompanied the Club last year, will be along, it is thought. He needs no introduction to those who had the pleasure of hearing him last year as he proved a favorite wherever he appeared. He will have an able helper in Mr. Ned Gregory, one of the students, who is a genius along theatrical lines.[12]

In an April article, *The Furman Hornet* writers detailed the entire tour, highlighting the more successful stops and memorable anecdotes of the students. The authors never fail to mention the effects of the Glee Club on the young women in attendance, and vice versa: "Two of our Club members came near leaving their hearts with two of Union's fairer sex. Probably they did, for through the remainder of the trip they were flirtation proof."[13] The next week the paper made special mention of Rhame's solo at the Glee Club concert given locally: "With his mellow voice he won the admiration of the entire house, and especially of the gallery, from which dropped, as if from the hand of one of the pleased gods of music, a beautiful red rose."[14]

In the following year began one of the traditions that marked the Glee Club's activities in the 1920s, hosting or participating in the South Carolina Intercollegiate Glee Club Contest. Drawing participants from all over South Carolina, including Wofford College, Clemson University, Presbyterian College, the University of South Carolina, and Newberry College, the contest involved singing a selection chosen by a panel of judges, selections of the club's choice, and each respective school's alma mater. The clubs also presented a combined selection, "The Winter Song" by F.F. Bullard and conducted by Schaefer.

The Glee Club's success at this contest would increase in later years, and the club continued to increase in popularity. Greenville seems to have taken notice of the Glee Club's success, for in 1924 the Greenville Chamber of Commerce sponsored the tour. The cover of the tour program reads, "The Chamber of Commerce of Greenville, S.C., appreciating the high position Furman University occupies in the educational advancement of the State, and also to Greenville as an institution, takes pleasure in introducing the Glee Club to the good people who patronize and encourage their program of entertainment."[15] The Chamber of Commerce utilized the program as an advertisement for Greenville's virtues both inside and outside the county, printing facts about Greenville on the reverse of the program. Most of these facts have to do with commercial endeavors, such as "The largest underwear manufacturing plant in the South," and "The largest inland cotton center in the United States." Some concern private assets of Greenville's citizenry, such as "Banking resources, $20,738,000." Still others have to do with infrastructure, weather, and amenities, such as "Average temperature for 12 months, 58.8 degrees," and "New 'Poinsett,' $1,000,000.00 twelve story hotel now under construction." Tours exposed the Glee Club and, through them, the university, to large audiences across wide areas of South Carolina and, occasionally, neighboring states. In addition to intermittent jaunts to neighboring cities, the spring tour involved several days of nearly non-stop performing. Under the direction of J. Oscar Miller, the 1925 tour, for example, involved 12 concerts in two weeks of travel.

In 1925 the Glee Club won the South Carolina Intercollegiate Glee Club Competition and went on to win the Southern Intercollegiate Glee Club Competition as well, earning the right to represent South Carolina in the national competition in New York. *The Baptist Courier* reported the club's success after a visit in March of the following year:

> The Glee Club of Furman University has had a great trip to the North. They did not, we believe, get the first prize in the competition, but they stood very high and were feasted by the Furman alumni of the City of New York. Upon their return through Washington they were presented to the President, and Mr. Coolidge stood with them for a picture. Also, they entertained an American audience over the radio. In every way it was a great trip for the boys, and worthwhile for Furman.[16]

Though they were unable to duplicate their feat in 1926, the Glee Club again won the Southern Intercollegiate Glee Club Competition in 1927. Travelling to New York City in the spring, they again sang on the radio for New York City audiences.

The Furman University Glee Clubs successes of 1925 and 1927 enhanced the ensemble's reputation to a considerable degree. The 1927 season's program is an elaborate creation, filled with pictures depicting the Glee Club, J. Oscar Miller (director), and officers of the club. The Glee Club won the Southern Intercollegiate Glee

Club Contest for their third and final time in the 1928 season, this time helping to make the contest an unusually large and well-attended event:

> [The] annual Southern Intercollegiate Glee Club contest... promises to be the largest event of its kind ever held in the South...Aside from the actual contest to determine the best college club in the South, with eight clubs competing, other musical features promise to make it an unparalleled event in Southern music. Feature of the night will be a chorus of one thousand male voices, which will be worked up under the leadership of Professor Miller, tutor of the present Southern champions, and DuPre Rhame, former Furman glee club star. Another feature of the contest will be a performance of the Clemson College symphony orchestra.
> The eight clubs to enter the contest will be the champions of their respective states, making the contest here a final event after a long process of elimination.[17]

The club's ambitions were not realized in terms of the number of participating schools or the size of the combined chorus, but the five schools who participated—Duke University, Furman University, the University of South Carolina, the University of Tennessee, and the University of Virginia—made a memorable showing. The Furman University Glee Club emerged as best of the clubs in attendance:

> By virtue of this victory in song, the Harmony Hurricane won the right to represent the South in the national contest to be held in New York in March, and also captured another

leg on the Southern cup to be retained permanently by the club winning it three times...A feature of the contest program was a grand chorus composed of the competing clubs, and other clubs of the state association including Wofford and Clemson, which rendered, under the direction of Professor Miller, "Bells of Saint Mary's" and "Prayer of Thanksgiving."[18]

Figure 3.6 – The front page of The Hornet, March 18, 1927. Photo courtesy Furman University Special Collections and Archives.

At the end of the 1920s, Nan Trammell Herring introduced another of Furman University's traditional songs to the campus. Her son, Gordon Herring, Furman University class of 1965, described his mother in an interview with the author:

Mother was born in 1907 and her parents moved to Greenville, where she spent the rest of her youth. She, like her mother, attended Greenville Woman's College. That was before, obviously, it became a part of Furman. She graduated in 1929 and then went from Furman to Cornell and got a master's degree in English, which was fairly uncommon for a young lady in those days.[19]

Nan Trammell Herring's interest in singing began as a young lady, on visits with her aunt, Mary Fanny Lanier:

> Mary Fanny was very proud of the fact that her husband was related to Sydney Lanier, the poet, but when Mother would spend some time with Mary Fanny, she would learn a lot of folk songs, because Mary Fanny was also very musically inclined. She played the organ at her church.[20]

The origin of the tune for Brown Eyes is unknown, and legends as to its meaning abounded on Furman University's campus. Beverly Simmons, writing in *The Furman Hornet* in 1959, on the song's thirtieth anniversary as a Glee Club favorite, gave an account of the song's popularity on campus:

> Around 1926 Nan Trammell Herring…sang it on a house party. The students were so impressed by it that they brought it back to Furman. Chip Owens and Arthur Smith…arranged it for their student orchestra. Because of its catchy folk tune and sentimental words, students liked it and soon it could be heard throughout the campus.
>
> It was picked up by the Boys' Glee Club who sang it while traveling from one concert to another during Spring Tour. Then each year when the tour came to a close and the boys returned to Furman it came to be traditional to sing it before leaving the bus.
>
> One year Mr. Rhame could not make the tour so he sent a student director. As an encore to a program this student

decided to use "Brown Eyes." It brought such a great and favorable response that Mr. Rhame arranged it for male voices and featured it on the tour program for several years.[21]

Dr. Gordon W. Blackwell, Furman University class of 1932 and president of the university from 1965 through 1976, in an effort to clarify the history of the beloved melody, researched the song's story and gave the following speech at a 1981 event on Furman University's campus, adding details to Simmons's account:

> The story of "Brown Eyes" as a Furman song begins more than fifty years ago. Nan Trammell '29, of Greenville, first heard Mrs. Jack West of nearby Belton sing the song. Nan recalls it as being an unwritten ballad. Arthur Smith '29, and Clifford A. "Chip" Owens '30, heard Nan sing "Brown Eyes," probably at a house party. Later Smith, who had a small combo called "Smith's Hot-footers," called Nan on the telephone and asked her to sing the song for him line by line while he wrote down the words and notes. He and Owens then orchestrated the song. That winter, 1928-29, Nan sang "Brown Eyes" with the combo at the half of a basketball game in the gymnasium on the former men's campus.
>
> Incidentally Nan and her husband, Alex Herring '32, are retired foreign missionaries now living in Greenville. Their three children are Furman graduates: James '57, Gordon '65, and Nancy Scott '69.
>
> The story of "Brown Eyes" continues. Programs by the Men's Glee Club in those years included several numbers by the instrumental combo and a men's trio. The spring tour in 1929 featured a singing trio of Arthur Smith,

now deceased; Chip Owens, now a retired executive of Prudential Life in Saint Simons Island, Georgia; and James Shelley '29, now a former Vice President of Merrill Lynch stockbrokers in Greensboro, North Carolina. The trio's first presentation of "Brown Eyes" was at Winthrop College. According to Chip, "The reception was enthusiastic everywhere we went." Also that spring the trio sang "Brown Eyes" over radio station WBTC in Charlotte, dedicating the rendition to Arthur's and Chip's girl friends, Elizabeth Johnston and Ella Little, respectively. Incidentally, singing on the radio in those days created some excitement since Greenville was not to have its own radio station until four years later.

Smith and Shelley graduated that year. The next year Chip Owens carried on as leader of the combo. "Brown Eyes" was kept alive by popular demand on the Glee Club tour and at dances where the combo played.

When professor DuPre Rhame became director of the Glee Club, he had "Brown Eyes" copyrighted. In more recent years it has been sung in concert and recorded by the Furman Singers. Each year freshmen learn the song and the tradition continues in numerous serenades on campus.

As Chip Owens has said, "None of us in 1929 could have foretold the remarkable future of 'Brown Eyes' at Furman. It never occurred to us then that we were witnessing a tradition being born." But now, 52 years later, we can all be grateful to Nan Trammell Herring, Arthur Smith, Chip Owens, and DuPre Rhame for bringing this beautifully plaintive song out of relative obscurity into a Furman tradition.[22]

Figure 3.7 – This portrait of Nan Trammell Herring hangs in the lobby of the Nan Trammell Herring Music Pavilion. Photo courtesy Furman Singers Archives.

Nan Trammell Herring was possessed of a beautiful voice, and frequently sang for fraternity functions. "Brown Eyes" was merely one of many songs she sang for such occasions. Gordon Herring relates that his mother "never really understood why one of the many, many songs that she learned as a child became so popular, but it kind of took on a life of its own."

Sarah Herring, wife of Gordon and Furman University class of 1966, believes that the song's function might have played a role in its popularity and durability: "Part of the appeal of 'Brown Eyes' was that it was a ballad, a love song, and it was used to serenade…it became sort of a theme, 'Brown Eyes, good night.'" [23]

The recipients of these evening serenades, the members of the Greenville Woman's College Glee Club, continued performances during these years and collaborated with the Furman University

Glee Club as well. In April of 1923 the clubs presented *The Rose Maiden*, a secular cantata by Frederich H. Cowen, featuring DuPre Rhame as the bass soloist. The following year, J. Oscar Miller, who directed both the Greenville Woman's College Glee Club and the Furman University Glee Club during that season, conducted a December 13 performance of Handel's *Messiah* at the Greenville Woman's College. *The Furman Hornet* announced that the performance would feature four soloists from Chicago. Large-scale performances of this sort remained a feature of the glee clubs' season each year, and performances of *Messiah* became a favorite of the glee clubs' directors and their audiences.

In 1929, on the edge of the Great Depression, Arnold E. Putman became the director of the Greenville Woman's College Glee Club. He would continue to direct the young women of the Greenville Woman's College and later Furman University for many years. David Parker conducted an interview with Mrs. Putman in 1987, in which she gave her account the couple's earliest experiences at the school:

> [Mr. Putman] graduated from Ithaca Conservatory of Music, and then he graduated with a B.S. degree from Ithaca. The agent he had was in Chicago that did most of the music professors. And so Put wrote to him and he gave him two jobs – and one was a religious school up in Evansville, Illinois: a place like Bob Jones [University, Greenville], that type of school; and the other was a temporary job at Shorter College in Rome, Georgia – because the [instructor at Shorter College] had gone to study and they wanted somebody to take her place while she was gone. And so Put took that, as against the other – but it was a long way from Duluth, Minnesota [the Putmans's home town]. But anyhow, we kept together and he came down and taught three years at Shorter.

> The last year, we were married and I came and was there that one year. Then the lady came back that they had promised, you see, so Put had to get a job. Well, it was in twenty-nine, and we talked to the man in Chicago and went to see places and whatnot, and finally we were just going to go home and stay with my mother 'till we could find something to do, and the man...wrote and said, 'You better go and see about a place in Greenville, South Carolina before you come North.' So Put got on the little choo-choo train and came over here and talked to Dr. Ramsey [president of the Greenville Woman's College] and Dr. Ramsey hired him right that morning, and Put said, 'Well, you don't have my credentials or anything.' 'We don't need them,' he [Dr. Ramsey] said, 'We want you.'
>
> Partly because he had me and the baby...and because they wanted a little family atmosphere – they wanted us to live on the first floor of the institution and be a family for the girls to feel at home with.[24]

The Greenville Woman's College, like most of the United States, was undergoing a period of extreme financial difficulty. It was also suffering from declining enrollment:

> The reason [Mr. Putman] took the job was we got our room and board free, which was invaluable in 1929. And so we lived in two little bedroom-type places on the first floor of the old institution, and ate in the dining room with all the girls. We did that for seven years, because the institution didn't have enough money to pay us in...1932, but we stayed there.
>
> We did have a place to sleep and the three meals, and we learned to like spinach whether we liked spinach or not.

Then Dr. Geer got us enough money to move out of the institution, so we bought a house on Augusta Road. But some of the faculty really had a lot of trouble those years. The school could hardly make it. One year we had only eighty-eight girls.

    Now this is my good story: Miss Thomas was the Dean of Women at the Woman's College, a beautiful person. She made that institution. So she got me in my car, and we went out all through Pickens and Easley. We'd look in the yards, and if there was a bale of cotton in the yard, we'd go in and say, "Do you have a high-school girl that would come to our institution?" And we got like ten or twelve pupils that way.[25]

The college also met with some difficulties in affording its faculty during these lean years, and Putman described her husband's creativity in finding the means to provide for his family:

> [Mr. Schaefer] said they couldn't afford Put's salary. He said, "you're only going to get the money that the girls pay in for voice lessons, that's all the money you're going to get." Well, you should have known old Put, he was furious. So he went out and collected himself some students, and he went and collected the money when they didn't pay, and he made more money than when they'd paid him salary, so they changed their mind.[26]

As the decade came to a close, the Greenville Woman's College faced more dire fiscal problems than Furman University. At the university, the building program, which had been very ambitious under President McGlothlin's leadership, largely came to a halt. Furman University received support for which the Greenville Woman's College could not hope, however, in the form of a five percent share of the $40,000,000 Duke Endowment, and through a series of proactive moves to control the school's debt, would weather the Great Depression.

The 1930s and the Return of a Glee Club Star

DuPre Rhame graduated in the spring of 1924 with a B.S. in physics from Furman University and a B.A. in music from the Greenville Woman's College. Over the course of the next six years, Rhame taught high school physics, toured for one year with a concert band in which he played percussion, and studied for a time at the Eastman School of Music. Eastman School of Music was a new institution in 1924, having been formed in 1921. Its founding took place in close proximity to the founding of the Juilliard Graduate School and the Curtis Institute of Music, both created in 1924. Rhame also visited his alma mater to work with the Glee Club before taking over as director of the Glee Club and the band in the fall of 1930.

Rhame continued the most prominent traditions of the club for a time, including participation in the Southern Intercollegiate Glee Club Contest in the spring of 1931. In the fall of 1930, however, he undertook a first-ever fall tour, and in the spring took the club to areas around both North and South Carolina. While in North Carolina the club visited Mars Hill College, North Carolina State Teacher's College, and performed in Asheville. Rhame also arranged a performance for radio station WWNC in Asheville. In the following years, Rhame continued to take the club on annual tours and perform in and around Greenville. In the fall of 1931 the club performed for United States Senator Walter F. George of Georgia, Georgia Governor Richard B. Russell, Jr., and South Carolina Governor Ibra C. Blackwood as part of the festivities surrounding the opening of the first paved highway from Mexico to Quebec. Rhame also directed the Furman University Band and undertook a joint tour of the two ensembles in the spring of 1936.

Fresh from his graduate experiences in New York, Rhame's repertoire selections reflect a more serious-minded approach to building a performance.

Figure 3.8 – DuPre Rhame. Photo courtesy Furman University Special Collections and Archives.

The membership of the club now numbered approximately thirty young men, and the concert programs were much more sober. Inside the cover of the 1930 program Rhame had the texts for the musical works printed. As mentioned in relation to "Brown Eyes," "Chip Owens and His Hot-Footers with Jack Barbeson" featured as part of the evening, recalling the almost vaudevillian character of the programs of the first thirty years of the club's history. Rhame also sang a solo, "The Trumpeter" by J. Airlie Dix and John Francis Barron. The program for the spring of 1931 also displays all the texts for the Glee Club's selections and moves notably toward the performance of art music, including selections by Frédéric Chopin, Ludwig Van Beethoven, and Arthur Sullivan. These programs set a pattern for the club that would characterize its performances throughout the 1930s.

Professor Arnold Putman continued to conduct the club at the Greenville Woman's College during the early part of the 1930s. The ties between the two schools' choral programs were formalized in the form of the Choral Club, a large mixed ensemble conducted by George Schaefer. An article in *The Furman Hornet* of 1932 describes the Choral Club; the article also mentions the already well-established expectation that the major oratorio of the Christmas season would be G.F. Handel's *Messiah*:

> The first rehearsal of the Choral Club, a musical organization of GSC, was held in the Fine Arts Auditorium last Tuesday night, under the direction of Professor Schaefer. Miss Bloss and Miss Lusby are the accompanists.
>
> The Choral Club is one of the outstanding features in extra-curricular activities at Greenville Woman's College. It is composed of all students who are studying music and any others interested in the work…This year in December the group will present Mendelssohn's *Elijah*. During the previous years it has been customary for the college musicians to present *The Messiah* by Handel, but it was deemed expedient by those in charge this year to change the Christmas oratorio.

> Professor Arnold E. Putman, well-known for his work during recent year in *The Messiah*, will take one of the solo parts in the oratorio.[27]

Attendance at the Greenville Woman's College had peaked in 1929, however, and, as mentioned above, the college was crippled by financial difficulties brought on by the advent of the Great Depression. The Greenville Woman's College began to coordinate its operations with Furman University in 1933. In 1938, the South Carolina Baptist Convention merged the two schools' administrations. For the choral organizations this meant combining for some functions, though the clubs retained their independent identities in the form of the Furman University Glee Club, under the direction of Rhame and Arnold Putman's Chapel Choir of Greenville Woman's College of Furman University, an unfortunate appellation, perhaps reflecting lingering sensitivity regarding the combination of the two institutions.

Enduring World War II

The latter part of the 1930s increased Furman University's debt to $200,000, but John Laney Plyler, seventh president of the university, took office on January 1, 1939, with a clear mandate to operate with deliberate, careful action to reduce the debt and stabilize the school's policies. Continued efforts at retrenchment became more difficult in the face of the deteriorating state of world politics. Japan attacked Pearl Harbor on December 7, 1941, and the United States declared war on Japan on December 8. Germany and Italy declared war on the United States on December 11, and the United States immediately declared war on them. This impacted Furman

University in a multitude of ways: supplies, ranging from travel essentials such as tires and gasoline to school needs such as paper and pencils were in short supply. Male enrollment dropped sharply. In response, Furman University increased its women's admissions. By May 1943, however, enrollment was only 40 percent of normal. Alice Putman recalled the difficulties of the war years:

> There were very few boys there…and the whole institution was just squashed for the time being. The Chapel Choir sang frequently for the war effort, especially in churches. They'd be doing drives for certain things and we'd sing for them. And we sang for this music club and that kind of thing. Yes, we did a good bit of singing around town, really.[28]

Carolyn Whatley Dennis, Furman University class of 1946, recalled the experience from a student's perspective:

> I started Furman in 1943, at 16 years of age, very young. We only had 11 grades in high school then. It was right in the middle of World War II. Mr. Rhame had always had a male glee club, and of course, the war took care of that for him. All the boys were gone.
>
> There were a few of us who were studying with Mr. Rhame, and we said, can't we just do some three-part harmony or something? So we developed this choral group called the Serenaders. We did a few things that small groups could do. We sang for the troops in the USO Building downtown, and (Mr. Rhame was a great Kiwanian) we sang often for the Kiwanis Club, and any other thing that he was asked to have a group to do, the Serenaders

did it for him. It was a very pleasant group, small, but we made pretty good music.[29]

Dennis also described the makeup of the Serenaders in terms of its personnel: "we weren't all voice students. I guess most of us were. I know Ellen Bridges was the pianist. She was a piano major. Everybody was in the music department. Everybody in the Serenaders was in some part of the music department."[30] Arnold Putman began a glee club for the female students of the university in 1940, sometimes titled a Girls' Glee Club and sometimes a Women's Glee Club in the *Bonhomie*.

No choral activity is on record for the 1943 to 1944 school year, and the 1944 to 1945 school year did not include a men's glee club. As noted above, Putman continued to direct the Girls' Glee Club, and Rhame continued to teach voice in addition to his new duties with students undergoing military training. The *Bonhomie* of 1945 paints a bittersweet picture of student life and the university's attempts at recovery:

> This year the girls went back to Montague, and the boys returned to Geer. Furman had the largest women's student body in its history. The draft continued to call Furman men into the service, yet the number of men students was larger than last year. The Furman University $2,000,000 Fund Campaign was launched under the direction of President Plyler. A few of the boys who had been in service returned to classes. Increased interest in student activities resulted in the reorganization of several clubs. Although indications are that Furman is gradually beginning to return to normalcy, the students on both campuses are aware, perhaps as never

before, that a war is on and that the day of victory is still in the future. It is for the purpose of the 1945 *Bonhomie* to show by pictures that in spite of the war, Furman students still have that intangible something we call school spirit.[31]

Male student enrollment shot up in the 1945-1946 school year. The *Bonhomie* picture of the Girls' Glee Club shows a large group of smiling young women, 53 in number. A few pages later, DuPre Rhame's new ensemble, mentioned above, is pictured, comprised of 18 women. There was no overlap between Rhame's Serenaders and Putman's Girls' Glee Club. The Boys' Glee Club had already boosted enrollment to 37 men. Though choral activity at Furman University had, in large part, returned to normalcy, the status quo could not remain. Soldiers returning from war and those who had remained desired something different from the musical structures they had known prior to World War II.

Figure 3.9 – DuPre Rhame and the Serenaders. Photo courtesy Furman University Special Collections and Archives.

1 Reid, 27.
2 "Harmony Hurricane Announces Tour Schedule," *Furman Hornet*, March 16, 1934.
3 Furman University. *Bonhomie*. (Greenville, South Carolina: 1901).
4 J. Perry White and George N. Heller. "Entertainment, Enlightenment, and Service: A History and Description of Choral Music in Higher Education." *College Music Symposium* 23, no. 2 (Fall, 1983): 10.
5 David Johnson, "The 18th-Century Glee," *The Musical Times* 120, no. 1633 (March, 1979): 200; "The Yale Glee Club: 1861-1961," *Music Educators Journal* 47, no. 6 (June-July, 1961): 81.
6 Furman University. *Bonhomie*. (Greenville, South Carolina: 1909).
7 "Furman's 'Alma Mater' Will Be Thirty Years Old Next Tuesday," *The Furman Hornet*, April 15, 1937.
8 "Concert By A.C. Club." *The Furman Hornet*, May 2, 1919.
9 Furman University. *Bonhomie*. (Greenville, South Carolina: 1919).
10 *Bonhomie*, 1924.
11 "Glee Club Making Rapid Progress," *The Furman Hornet*, February 25, 1922.
12 *The Furman Hornet*, February 25, 1922.
13 "A Brief Review of the Furman Glee Club – Day By Day," *The Furman Hornet*, April 15, 1922.
14 "Furman Glee Club and Purple Stringers Orchestra Give Delightful Entertainment," *The Furman Hornet*, April 22, 1922.
15 Furman University. *Furman Glee Club*. Concert Program. 1924; Furman University. *Bonhomie*. (Greenville, South Carolina: 1924).
16 "Editorial and Personal," *The Baptist Courier*, March 18, 1926.
17 "Southern Glee Club Contest Here Soon," *The Furman Hornet*, January 24, 1928.
18 "Purple Songsters Win Second Southern Contest," *The Furman Hornet*, February 14, 1928.
19 Gordon and Sarah Herring, interview by author, May 9, 2011, Greenville, South Carolina, Digital Recording.
20 Herring, interview.
21 Beverly Simmons. "'Brown Eyes' First Sung Years Ago," *The Furman Hornet*, October 17, 1959.
22 Gordon Blackwell. "A History of Brown Eyes." *Furman University*. (Greenville, South Carolina: 1981).
23 Herring, interview.
24 Alice Putman, quoted in Parker, 10-11.
25 Alice Putman, quoted in Parker, 11-12.
26 Alice Putman, quoted in Parker, 12.
27 "Choral Club Has First Practice," *The Furman Hornet*, October 28, 1932.
28 Alice Putman, quoted in Parker, 14.
29 Carolyn Whatley Dennis, interview by author, June 2, 2011, Greenville, SC, Digital Recording.
30 Dennis, interview.
31 Furman University. *Bonhomie*. (Greenville, South Carolina: 1945).

CHAPTER 4

DUPRE DIRECTED ME: THE TENURE OF DUPRE RHAME

The Founding of the Furman Singers and Rhythms of the School Year

Rhame enjoyed working with the Serenaders and knew, even before the 1946 to 1947 school year had begun, that he wanted to create a mixed ensemble, the first of its kind on Furman University's campus. The students were in agreement with him and expressed their feelings on the matter in the spring and summer of 1946. Carolyn Dennis described the events surrounding the founding of Furman Singers to David Parker:

> Some of the men came in during the last semester of 1945, and of course [Rhame] was just getting them in dribbles. He didn't have enough for a male glee club, and some of us didn't want him to do that because we had a little taste of this and didn't want to give it up. So, by the fall there were lots of men back.
> I remember very distinctly the meeting that he called, and we met in the chapel on the men's campus, the men's old campus, and there were so many people...I can't tell you how many there were...Well, that was our organizational meeting, and [Rhame] had a list of names that he wanted to kick around that night to see what we wanted to call this group. Of course, some of the people that had been in the Serenaders were very

strong to keep that name, but we finally, after a lot of debate, zeroed in on Furman Singers, that very first day.[1]

DuPre Rhame immediately recognized the potential of the ensemble and it became the focus of his efforts. The students of the club elected Dennis their first president, who emphasized the *esprit de corps* already present in the group:

> [I did] just the usual things that presidents do: try to make sure you talked to everybody…of course we didn't have much problem, everybody was so glad to be back, the boys especially. There was a camaraderie in that group, and it's amazing, because it's still there today. It's gone through every generation. It was an easy job for me.[2]

In the wake of the formation of Furman Singers, the Men's Glee Club continued for a time, but membership overlap between the two ensembles was nearly complete and Rhame dissolved the Glee Club in 1949. Remarkably, the 1946 to 1947 season became a template for most of the history of Furman Singers. Dennis briefly described that year:

> That first year, we had no tour, but we did all the things you usually do – we did concerts, the conventions, we did the Kiwanis [Club] – everything that [Rhame] was involved in. Plus the *Messiah*, which we had done every year anyway… We did the first operetta that [Rhame] did with the Furman Singers in the spring of 1947. It was Herbert's *Sweethearts*.[3]

Though, as Dennis mentioned, there was no tour in 1947, by the spring of 1948 the annual tour had resumed, and Furman Singers began the process of establishing a musical reputation in the area around Greenville. The concerts, conventions, and Kiwanis performances to which Dennis alluded were a part of every year. Concerts on campus included incidental performances for university functions, such as spring commencement, Founders' Day, and a spring concert, usually following tour.

By 1949 Furman Singers had become the center of the musical life of the university. The spring concert of that year was an elaborate affair and included collaboration with the Southern Symphony Orchestra and Carl Bamberger, its conductor. The concert was broadcast on 14 South Carolina radio stations. Christina Carroll, a soprano who had sung roles in *Carmen*, *La Boheme,* and other operas with the Metropolitan Opera from 1943 through 1946, was a guest soloist.

Figure 4.1 – Furman University Singers and DuPre Rhame, 1948. Photo courtesy Furman Singers Archives.

Among the more important developments of the 1950s was the construction of an entirely new campus for Furman University on the outskirts of Greenville. For Furman Singers this meant that rehearsals and performances shifted from First Baptist Church and the former site of the Greenville Woman's College to the new campus. Initial plans for the expansion and relocation coincided with the end of World War II and escalating enrollment, thanks to heightened admissions numbers for non-veteran females and returning veterans. The groundbreaking for the new campus took place in October of 1953, and the move to the new campus began with the freshmen men, who settled into the freshly completed dormitories in the fall of 1955. McAlister Auditorium, home of Furman Singers for most of its major concerts, was completed in the fall semester of 1960 and the building was dedicated on November 4 of that year.

Figure 4.2 – McAlister Auditorium.

Once this move was complete, Furman Singers rehearsed in this new space once each week and two days each week in Plyler Hall, the new science building. These rehearsals took place in Townes Lecture Auditorium, one of the few classrooms on campus large enough to seat the ensemble comfortably. Lloyd Linney, a member of Furman Singers and Furman University class of 1970, remembers rehearsals as one of the most enjoyable aspects of participation in Furman Singers: "Rehearsals were something I just wouldn't think of missing. I just loved being in Singers and I loved rehearsing under [Rhame]. He had such a way of drawing you in."[4] Chapel performances and chapel attendance were a regular part of university life, and Singers performed for chapel each Thursday. Gordon and Sarah Herring recalled the chapel programs in an interview with the author:

> Sarah Herring: We practiced on Tuesdays and Thursdays, and we sang for chapel on those days. The Tuesday program was secular, informational, but the Thursday program was actually a chapel service. It was mandatory, not just for Singers but for all the students. The seat checker would sit up in the balcony...
> Gordon Herring: You had to sit in an assigned seat, and they would check the empty seats and see who didn't make it to chapel.
> Sarah Herring: And so you couldn't graduate if you had missed too many times at chapel. You had a very limited number of cuts from chapel.[5]

Performances for civic groups such as the Kiwanis Club of Greenville, with whom Rhame remained active throughout his life, and events associated with the South Carolina Baptist Convention accounted for much of the yearly activity of Furman Singers. The South Carolina Baptist Convention's location shifted from year to year. It was sometimes held in Greenville, but was often held in Columbia or Charleston, which meant longer travel and occasionally overnight stays.

The First Concert of the Year: Handel's *Messiah*

One of the highlights of each year was the Christmas performance of G.F. Handel's *Messiah,* which was, even in 1946, a well-established tradition. Professor George Schaefer had presented *Messiah* as a joint effort of the Furman University Glee Club and the

Greenville Woman's College when Rhame was a student. Rhame recalled those performances fondly and decided to reintroduce the oratorio to Greenville when he returned to Furman University as a faculty member. His first presentation of *Messiah* was in 1935 with the Buncombe Street United Methodist Church Choir and a few Furman University students. He was the musical director of Buncombe Street, and in that first performance the ensemble numbered 35, scarcely more than a tenth the size of Rhame's largest ensembles for *Messiah* presentations.

Rhame became the director of music at the First Baptist Church of Greenville the next year, and after 1935, renditions of *Messiah* continued without interruption, even through World War II. Rhame recalled that military personnel from the Greenville Army Air Base helped "make up for the lack of male students" on Furman's campus in the 1945 concert. In addition to Furman Singers, performances involved Furman University's Concert Choir after its formation in 1958, church members from First Baptist, Furman alumni, and the Greenville community at large.[6] The orchestra and chorus tended to be massive, sometimes numbering more than 300. As Carolyn Dennis recalled, "Everybody in Greenville who could sing and wanted to be in it was in it. It was beautiful music."[7]

In addition to the spectacle of the enormous chorus and instrumental ensemble, Rhame preferred soloists who were part of the Furman faculty, singers from the community, or professionals. He believed that the difficulty of the solos required performers possessed of more vocal maturity than the undergraduates. Jerry Langenkamp, who joined the faculty in 1960 as a voice teacher and conductor of the newly formed Concert Choir, performed the tenor solos for several years during his ten-year tenure at the school. Shirley Duncan, alto, and Sidney Buckley, bass, both of whom were instructors at Furman University, were also soloists on several occasions. An organ prelude of varied selections often preceded the oratorio, performed for many years by Lindsay Smith, another instructor at Furman University. The involvement of so many people helped make the performance a community event.

This tradition, the yearly performance of a single, large-scale work to a packed house, puzzled Jerry Langenkamp when he arrived at Furman University. He described his first experience with Rhame's *Messiah* concerts to David Parker:

> Well, the performance was to be at three o'clock, but McAlister was absolutely full by two. I remember I was sitting next to John Crabtree, and that's where I met him, in fact. We were behind the curtain, and DuPre was standing in front of us, talking to us. For some reason, the curtain started to go up. Well, DuPre turned to the stage manager and yelled, "Stop!" Just then, all the lights in the auditorium blew out. We sat there talking in the dark, and the lights didn't come back on for an hour and fifteen minutes. Finally, after all that time, the lights came up and the orchestra tuned. Well, when the curtain came up, not a soul had left that auditorium. Every single seat was taken.[8]

Part of the explanation of the performance's continued popularity must have been its dual role as a musical happening and homecoming. Lloyd Linney described the event's reunion character:

> When we did *Messiah* it was always Furman Singers and Concert Choir and then some people from town who wanted to do it. For instance, my brother kept coming back even when he wasn't a member of Furman Singers. The whole time he was at Furman he would always come back and sing

in *Messiah*, and even came back when I was a student after he had gone to medical school. That was just such a traditional thing. We would do it on a Sunday afternoon in the first weekend in December or something and McAlister auditorium was always packed with people.[9]

Rhame was aware of and enjoyed this aspect of the performance, as well as the sheer size of the event:

"I had no idea that the *Messiah* would grow to such proportions, or would become such a tremendous and involved production here...But had I known, I would most certainly have done it anyhow, for it has been a wonderfully rewarding experience, with just one purpose – to bring the *Messiah* to Greenville audiences."[10]

Spring Tour

After the end of fall semester and Christmas break, Rhame and Furman Singers shifted focus to the spring tour. As discussed in the previous chapter, tours with Furman's choruses, both locally and nationally, have been part of the fabric of the school year since the earliest days of the Furman University Glee Club. Though Furman Singers did not tour in the first year of its existence, Rhame reinstituted the spring tour the following year. *The Furman Hornet* announced 1948's travels:

Covering approximately 1,150 miles and traveling through North and South Carolina, the Furman University Singers will leave on January 26th for a tour which will last almost two weeks, Director DuPre Rhame of the Music Department announced this week. This will be the first time in the history of the school that a mixed group of this sort has taken such a tour. Mr. Rhame stated that he hoped to make this an annual event for the Singers.[11]

Stops included several locations in South Carolina as well as Raleigh, Durham, Winston Salem, and Charlotte. Concerts took place in school auditoriums and churches; Rhame set a tough schedule for the ensemble, with performances each day. Another *Hornet* article reviewed the Greenville concert that followed the tour. The student author made special mention of selections from Gilbert and Sullivan's *The Gondoliers*, the "Whiffenpoof Song," and "Dry Bones." Much to the audience's delight, Rhame included Fred Waring's "weird clicks, bone snaps, and other ghostly gyrations" in the last selection.

Figure 4.3 – From left to right, Jerry Langenkamp, DuPre Rhame, and Gayle Gulley on tour. Photo courtesy Furman Singers Archives.

Tours in subsequent years followed much the same pattern, though the tour varied in terms of timing with regard to the school calendar due to its coincidence with the Easter holiday. This meant departing on Palm Sunday and returning on Easter Sunday, watching friends depart for Spring Break as Furman Singers stayed in the dorms until time to leave. The ensemble traveled in two tour buses, and Rhame traveled in one but needed a chaperone for the second bus. For many years that duty fell to Agnes Martin, an employee of the admissions department of the university who first began traveling with Furman Singers so that she could reach the South Carolina Baptist Convention. Rhame asked Martin to continue helping with tour by supervising the second bus of students, and she quickly became a favorite of Furman Singers, adding her homemade cookies to the tour's travel experience. Though travel by bus was not a glamorous affair, Rhame's careful planning usually made it uneventful, at least. In 25 years of touring with Rhame, Furman Singers seldom arrived late for concerts or suffered through unnecessarily long days of confinement on the vehicles. Agnes Martin recalled one of the few travel-related mishaps to befall Furman Singers:

> I remember once, about the second or third tour I went on, we sang in Greenwood on Sunday afternoon and then had to be in Lancaster by five o'clock. We were on a Queen City Lines bus, chartered to Trailways, and one of our two buses broke down between Greenwood and Lancaster. They thought maybe they could get it fixed.
> So the first bus went on ahead, but first we stopped and put the music and all the soloists on the first bus. I was on the second bus. They were hoping to get [our bus] fixed and

bring us on in. And they didn't get it fixed, and we sat there and sat there until nightfall, and they unloaded the [first bus] and that driver came back and picked us up.

So we got there after the service, but the other half of the choir did the concert the best they could, since they had the music and the soloists. That's really the worst misfortune I can remember us having; tour usually went so smoothly.[12]

Gordon Herring was a senior manager for Furman Singers, and remembers the chores of stuffing robes into boxes and hauling the boxes and risers onto and off the buses. Sarah Herring reminisced about the change that the ensemble underwent from robes to formal wear, and the difficulties that change presented the women of Furman Singers:

In those days the women wore formals that they provided themselves for tours, and in the 60s the fashion was that you had multiple slips and petticoats. You couldn't get as many people on the riser with all their formal dresses on as you could when you had everybody crammed in robes. And that became a challenge for the managers to make sure that we could place everybody, because not only the packing was a hassle, but all of these skirts had to have multiple ruffles... You had your formal that you got out to put on every night and it really started to be ramshackle by the end of tour. But we would wear robes for the sacred part of the tour and then take off robes and then be in the looking-more-faded formals by the end of the week.[13]

Figure 4.4 – Mr. and Mrs. Rhame on tour in 1967. Photo courtesy Lloyd Linney.

Rhame structured the tour concerts in such a way that they could be adapted to the varied audiences for whom Furman Singers performed. He categorized each tour stop's concert as either of a general (mix of secular and sacred) character or sacred character, and segmented the concert into parts that could be performed independently or as a whole. A much more detailed discussion of repertoire for tours may be found in Chapter 6 of this document.

During DuPre Rhame's tenure, spring tour did not venture outside the southeastern United States until 1970, the last year Rhame directed the Furman Singers. Rhame decided to make his last tour a trip that included New York City as a stop, though all remaining stops were in the southeast. The concert in New York City took place in the Georgian Room of the Piccadilly Hotel. The audience for the occasion was comprised of Furman University alumni and their guests. Letters from various Furman University officials and alumni heralded the event, including a letter from Rhame himself. Richard Pollock, president of the New York Area Chapter of the Furman University Alumni Association, penned two letters encouraging the chapter's membership to attend the concert, the first of which praised Rhame and discussed his impending retirement:

> Having served Furman University for forty-five years (1925-1970) as professor of music, director of the Fine Arts, conductor of the Glee Club, the Serenaders, and founder and conductor of the Furman University Singers, DuPre Rhame, Furman's renowned "Master of Music," comes to the milestone of retirement at the end of the current school year. Known throughout the Southeast for their superb performances, Furman University Singers has become one of the finest and best-known college choral groups in that area. We are indeed fortunate that New York City is included on their annual spring tour this year…The buffet dinner is the best in town! We may have selections from six meats with all the trimmings – price - $7.50 per plate.[14]

The New York alumni also received a mailing including a short note from Pollock and a letter from Richard W. Riley, Furman University class of 1954 and President of the Furman University Alumni

Association. Riley would later become governor of South Carolina. After the performance at the Piccadilly Hotel, Rhame gave the students a day in the city to sightsee before boarding the bus to their next stop in Richmond, Virginia.

Jerry Langenkamp, in the two final years of Rhame's time directing Furman Singers, conducted a small ensemble within Furman Singers. Langenkamp, as mentioned above, came to Furman University to conduct the Concert Choir, an ensemble founded in 1959 by Thomas Redcay, a member of the piano faculty. The mission of Concert Choir was to perform sacred repertoire of the highest quality. Unlike Furman Singers, which was a large ensemble open to anyone interested in singing, Concert Choir was an auditioned group whose membership remained around 40 and was comprised of music majors. Langenkamp took a sabbatical during the 1967 to 1968 school year and, in his absence, Furman University restructured the choral music faculty, hiring Milburn Price to conduct the Concert Choir and making Langenkamp DuPre Rhame's associate conductor. Rhame allowed Langenkamp to create a small ensemble of approximately 16 Furman Singers that sang on tours in 1969 and 1970. Lloyd Linney and Bingham Vick, Jr., in conversations with the author, expressed the opinion that Rhame was grooming Langenkamp to replace him as director of Furman Singers.[15] The repertoire of Chamber Singers consisted of pieces of music suited to a small ensemble of mixed voices, including madrigals, motets, contemporary choral works, and hymn arrangements by Robert Shaw and Alice Parker.

The Spring Opera

As soon as Furman Singers returned from the spring tour, preparations for the last major performance of the year began. DuPre Rhame was a talented bass, a frequent soloist, and a lover of opera. His love for opera and operetta took shape in staged spring productions with Furman Singers serving as chorus. In the latter part of the 1940s Rhame explored the operettas of Gilbert and Sullivan, including *The Gondoliers* (1947), *H.M.S. Pinafore* (1948), and *The Mikado* (1949). These performances were presented at the Ramsay Fine Arts Auditorium of the Greenville Woman's College until the aforementioned move to McAlister in 1960. Students performed all of the roles in Rhame's early productions.

Figure 4.5 – Rhame in rehearsal in McAlister Auditorium.
Photo courtesy Furman Singers Archives.

In the 1950s Rhame programmed a variety of operettas, including *Naughty Marietta* (1954), with music by Victor Herbert and libretto by Rida Johnson Young; *The Three Musketeers* (1955), with music by Rolf Friml and libretto by P.G. Wodehouse and Clifford Grey; *The Bartered Bride* (1956), with music by Bedrich Smetana and libretto by Karel Sabina; *Robin Hood* (1957), with music by Reginald de Koven and libretto by Harry B. Smith; and *The Gipsy Baron* (1958), with music by Johann Strauss and libretto by Ignatius

Schnitzer.[16]   Rhame returned to Gilbert and Sullivan in 1959 with another performance of *H.M.S. Pinafore*. Furman student Rose V. Sims reviewed the production in *The Furman Hornet* of March 7, 1959: "The Furman University Singers presented the light operetta to a receptive audience that all but filled the house for a rainy opening night...Backed up by a mixed chorus that more or less sang its heart out, four university students stepped into the spotlight with leading parts in the production."[17] By 1959 Rhame had been directing the spring opera for more than a decade, and in an article on the same page, DuPre Rhame remembered past mishaps in the opera productions, including a lead soprano with the measles, a lead who was forced to perform with a sprained ankle (and a cane), and a scripted swordfight fall that resulted in a broken arm.

The 1960 production of *M'lle Modiste*, with music by Victor Herbert and libretto by Henry Blossom, attracted a great deal of student attention on Furman University's campus. Rhame double-cast the lead role with two freshmen, Janet McGee and Linda Lee, and utilized a chorus of approximately 60 Furman Singers, which, a student reviewer for *The Furman Hornet* remarked, lent "character to the music and gayness to the production."[18] In 1961 Rhame returned to one of his productions from the 1940s: Victor Herbert's *Sweethearts*. *Sweethearts* featured a wealth of extra-musical attractions, including instrumental music provided by the Furman Band, several comedic character roles, and a performance by the members of the Pershing Rifles Scabbard and Blade, who provided precision military drill movements for the production. The performance was well attended and merited a lengthy review in *The Furman Hornet*, including descriptions of the audience:

> Two audiences, each of well over a thousand persons, saw and applauded the Furman Singers' performance of the Victor Herbert operetta "Sweethearts" on May 12 and 13...

The song, "Pilgrims of Love," which followed, and the weird dance routine incorporated into the song brought fully as many laughs as the lyrics.

During the first half of the production, the audience seemed a little restless in the serious scenes. The voices of the six sisters were too light to be heard over the orchestra, and at times even Julie Martin could not be heard over the accompaniment...Hidden microphones used during the second part of the operetta remedied this situation, however.

The chorus was good, and the songs in which it was used had a certain spark of life about them...Two equally indefatigable personalities, Professor DuPre Rhame and Dr. Dorothy Richey, were the music and production directors. The work evidenced a wonderful job by both of them. Through the years they have gained a reputation for the high quality of their direction, and that reputation was upheld by the performances this year.[19]

The production came at the close of Rhame's interest in staging operetta with Furman Singers. Rhame's attention turned to grand opera in the 1960s.

In 1963 DuPre Rhame brought George Bizet's *Carmen* to McAlister Auditorium. Rather than casting students in the lead roles, Rhame hired professional singers from the Metropolitan Opera Company, the Chicago Lyric Opera, and elsewhere to fill the title role and a few others. The impressive cast included Nell Rankin, who sang the role of Carmen, Irene Callaway, who sang the role of Micaèla, Richard Cassilly, who sang the role of Don Jose, and Norman Treigle, who sang the role of Escamillo. Jerry Langenkamp sang the role of el Remendado. The student cast numbered over 100 and was comprised of students from Furman Singers and

Concert Choir. They sang choruses and performed dances as part of the production. Gordon and Sarah Herring participated in *Carmen*, both as chorus members and as part of the production crew. Gordon Herring shared a memory of one of the more tense moments in the production:

> I had helped a little with the set, and the drama department produced those. I forget the professor's name, but it was a scene with a forest and in-between acts... he realized that we had not trimmed the canvas to make it look like leaves, and so we lowered that part and we were there cutting away at the canvas to keep it from looking like just a straight line... It extended the intermission a lot longer than DuPre was happy with.[20]

Sarah Herring noted that, although moments in the performance might have been less than professional, "our hearts were in the right place."

Rhame followed this production with a string of grand opera performances in the following four years. These included Charles Gounod's *Faust* (1964), Giuseppe Verdi's *La Traviata* (1965), Ambroise Thomas's *Mignon* (1966), and Verdi's *Il Trovatore* (1967). Just as with the Furman Singers *Messiah* performances, in each case Rhame hired professional singers to perform the more demanding solo work employed Furman Singers as understudies and joined the remaining students with Concert Choir in the chorus. The exceptionally large budget required for these productions was made possible, at least in part, by Rhame's role as Chair of the Furman University Music Department. In 1968 and 1969 Rhame downsized the spring collaborations between Furman University's orchestra and choral departments to un-staged oratorio performances. Furman Singers presented Franz Joseph Haydn's *The Creation* in

1968 and Felix Mendelssohn's *Elijah* in 1969. In each case the same faculty who performed solos as part of the Furman Singers presentation of Handel's *Messiah* sang the soprano, alto, tenor, and bass solos. This included Jerry Langenkamp as the tenor soloist.

Just as with the Furman Singers trip to New York City in 1970, Rhame, planning for his impending retirement that spring, hoped to do something exceptional for his final spring presentation. He settled on a massive production of Giuseppe Verdi's *Aida*. Again Rhame secured stellar professional singers for the performance. Ella Lee sang the title role, Beverly Wolff sang the role of Amneris, and Jerry Langenkamp sang the role of Radames. Just as with prior productions, students understudied the roles and sang with orchestra before the arrival of the professional singers. The entire music department participated in preparations for the performance, which took place on Friday, April 24 at 8:15 pm in McAlister. Dr. Gordon W. Blackwell, Furman University's president, addressed a letter to all former Furman Singers, inviting them to the opera as well as the reception on Sunday morning in the Burgiss Lounge of the Watkins Student Center as part of Furman University's DuPre Rhame Day. The reception was followed by a luncheon in the Charles E. Daniel Dining Hall.

Impressions of DuPre Rhame

The institutional identity of Furman Singers from 1946 through 1970 was and is inextricably bound up in the identity of its director through those years. DuPre Rhame was an impressive physical presence, possessed of a fine bass-baritone voice, and a powerful personality. He seldom left those acquainted with him without an opinion of him. Charles Brock, former president of Furman Singers and Furman University class of 1956, spoke to David Parker of his memories of DuPre Rhame:

The Furman Singers

Figure 4.6 – This portrait of DuPre Rhame hangs in the lobby of the Herring Music Pavilion. Photo courtesy Furman Singers Archives.

I'm not at all sure that my impression of Mr. Rhame changed from the legendary figure that I'd heard about before coming to Furman, the rather dynamic personality that he had certainly held true all the way through my four years of being fairly close to him…I think he was sort of the embodiment of the power I always felt in music, and he had this very dominant trait about him on what good music was and what kind of work it required to make good music…Very demanding, and demanding not only in the manner in which he wanted the sound to be, but very demanding in loyalty…There was very little he could not have gotten us to do.[21]

Carolyn Dennis, who was his student but also a close family friend for many years, noted, "When he was directing he had a way of just pulling you with him. My husband always said to me that if Mr. Rhame asked you to walk on the water, [you] would try."[22] Lloyd Linney knew him as a voice instructor and as director of Furman Singers:

> He was a very warm person. He was kind of halfway in age between my grandfather and my own father, both of whom were very important in my life, and he kind of split that right in the middle. He was a fatherly image to me. I very much looked up to him, always wanted to please him. He was always very warm and very approachable.[23]

Bingham Vick, Jr., who took Rhame's place as conductor of Furman Singers in the fall of 1970, remembers Rhame as "bigger than life," with a "booming baritone voice" and imposing presence. He also shared memories of Rhame's understanding of the delicacy of Vick's position during his first years as conductor of Furman Singers: "DuPre never tried to look over my shoulder. He knew that Singers was in good hands when I came, and he also was wise enough to understand that some things would be different, and that was ok."[24] Rhame left an indelible mark on Furman University through his 40 years as a member of the music faculty. His work with the Furman Singers remains a central, vital part of that legacy.

1 Dennis, quoted in parker, 17.
2 Dennis, interview.
3 Dennis, quoted in Parker, 17.
4 Lloyd Linney, phone interview by author, June 4, 2011, Digital Recording.
5 Gordon and Sarah Herring, interview.
6 Dennis, interview; Bingham Vick, Jr., interview by author, April 18, 2011, Greenville, South Carolina, Digital Recording.
7 Dennis, interview.
8 Langencamp, quoted in Parker, 29.
9 Linney, interview.
10 Cheatham.
11 "FU Singers Begin Tour January 26," The Furman Hornet, January 10, 1948.
12 Agnes Martin, quoted in Parker, 30.
13 Gordon and Sarah Herring, interview.
14 Richard Pollock, letter to the New York Area Chapter of the Furman University Alumni Association, undated. Furman Singers Archives, Furman University, Greenville, South Carolina.
15 Linney, interview; Vick, interview, April 18, 2011.
16 Naughty Marietta. Concert program. Furman Singers Archives. (Greenville, South Carolina: 1954); The Three Musketeers. Concert program. Furman Singers Archives. (Greenville, South Carolina: 1955); The Bartered Bride. Concert program. Furman Singers Archives. (Greenville, South Carolina: 1956); Robin Hood. Concert program. Furman Singers Archives. (Greenville, South Carolina: 1957); The Gipsy Baron. Concert program. Furman Singers Archives. (Greenville, South Carolina: 1958).
17 Rose V. Sims. "Operetta Lively, Colorful," The Furman Hornet, March 7, 1959.
18 Beth George. "Female Leads Perform Well in Operetta," The Furman Hornet, March 12, 1960.
19 David Tomlinson. "Character Parts Steal Show in Operetta," The Furman Hornet, May 20, 1961.
20 Gordon and Sarah Herring, interview.
21 Charles Brock, quoted in Parker, 21.
22 Dennis, interview.
23 Linney, interview.
24 Bingham Vick, Jr., in an email to the author, June 3, 2011.

CHAPTER 5

I SING FOR BING: THE TENURE OF BINGHAM VICK, JR.

Bingham Vick, Jr. and a Handbook for Excellence

By 1970, DuPre Rhame had been planning for retirement for several years. Rhame had a clear successor in Jerry Langenkamp, someone who knew Furman Singers and was known and liked by students. Unfortunately, both Langenkamp's and his wife's parents fell ill toward the end of the 1960s. Both sets of parents lived in Kansas, and Langenkamp, hearing of an opening at Kansas State University, applied for a professorship there. This left Furman University's administration with a difficult search for someone to take Rhame's place.[1]

Bingham Vick, Jr. applied for the position through a contact, Lindsay Smith. Vick believes it to be likely that Furman University's administration and Rhame felt comfortable with him because of the similarities between Furman University and Vick's alma mater, Stetson University in Florida. A native of Charlotte, North Carolina, Vick earned a Bachelor of Arts degree in music from Stetson University, then studied vocal performance at Northwestern University. He earned a master's degree in performance then went on to study music history and literature, earning a Ph.D. after becoming a part of Furman University's faculty. While at Northwestern University, Vick studied with Margaret Hillis and served as assistant conductor for the Chicago Symphony Chorus.

Vick was 26 years old when he came to Furman University, and his age and experience contrasted sharply with that of DuPre Rhame. Vick made a strong impression on students, however, immediately projecting competence and maturity. Rhame eased the transition process by being present to guide Vick through the procedures he had helped establish over 25 years of leadership, but allowing Vick room to make his own decisions regarding the ensemble. Rhame also helped Vick settle into life in Greenville, sponsoring Vick's membership application to the Kiwanis Club. Over the course of the next several years, Rhame and wife Eleanor became fast friends with the younger conductor and his wife, Judy Vick.

Figure 5.1 – Bingham Vick, Jr., in 1970. Photo courtesy Furman Singers Archives

In many ways, Vick continued the practices of DuPre Rhame. Inevitably, however, the change in leadership meant some changes in Furman Singers, and among the most obvious signs of change are the ensemble overview pamphlets of 1969, 1970, and 1971. The 1969 and 1970 pamphlets are fairly straightforward and plain. Each of them pictures McAlister Auditorium on the front cover, above which is printed "The Furman University Singers Welcome You to Furman." On the inside front cover is a picture of Furman Singers in McAlister's lobby, and below is a message of welcome from the president of Furman Singers. In 1969 the pictures accompanying the pamphlet include rather somber shots of the *Aida* performances, Furman Singers on stage, and the officers. The pamphlet for 1970 includes a headshot of Vick, but remains largely unchanged. The 1971 pamphlet cover, far different from prior years' publications, is a collage of pictures from the 1970-1971 school year's tour and social events, and it admonishes the prospective Furman Singer to "Try a little happiness." In the center of the collage are pictured Bingham and Judy Vick along with their new puppy. Sandra Melton, the president of Furman Singers, includes a welcome similar to her predecessor, but concludes with the message that Furman Singers is a "lively group of college students who love to sing and love to have fun."[2]

In addition to this pamphlet, Furman Singers began publishing a handbook for participation in the 1970s. Vick modeled the handbook on and borrowed heavily from the Northwestern University choral ensemble handbook.[3] The handbook provides a short history of Furman Singers and the new Furman Singer is assured that, "as a member of Furman Singers, you automatically become a part of not only this fine choral tradition, but also a part of the long-lasting Furman tradition that the Singers have upheld through the years." In it, Vick details the core values of the ensemble:

> This group of people is far more than just a chorus. Those who have been a part of Singers for several years will attest to the personal enjoyment and pride that can be yours. If

you will apply yourself, keeping the Singers moving toward excellence in music and, just as important, growth, maturity, and fulfillment as individuals, you will soon realize how truly satisfying and exciting the Furman Singers is.[4]

Vick also systematically outlines the policies and administration of the ensemble, including attendance, membership, and dress.
The handbook contains some basic musical vocabulary and a paragraph admonishing the singer to listen, watch, and count, with specific instructions for good rehearsal technique. This somewhat cumbersome paragraph would later evolve into more concise rules of musicianship. By the fall of 1988, Vick had pared down the language of the handbook to five rules:

Rule #1 – No note value (volume) remains constant. Sound is moving!
Rule #2 – All same notes are not created equal!
Rule #3 – Always breathe for phrase (not for air).
Rule #4 – All consonants have an exact correct place in time.
Rule #5 – Always be expressive (tone quality, energy, facially).[5]

Vick eventually shortened this list to three simple statements: "Rule #1: Never sustain the same volume. Rule #2: No two adjacent notes get the same stress. Rule#3: Always make music."[6] These rules became a prominent part of Vick's rehearsals, serving to communicate quickly and efficiently the principles of musicianship Vick valued in his singers.

Though Furman Singers did not include a constitution in its handbook, the Furman Band did, for at least a limited period, and Vick modeled a constitution for Furman Singers on the Furman

Band's example. The Furman Singers constitution offers a somewhat more detailed account of the officer structure in the 1970s:

> Officers for this organization shall consist of a President, Vice President, treasurer, two secretaries, and two historians elected by the members of the organization each year. Also included in the officers, but not elected, shall be an accompanist, appointed by the conductor, and three managers. The Managers shall consist of one Head Manager who is the Senior Manager and two assistant managers. Managers shall hold their positions for three years, beginning in the sophomore year and continuing through the Senior year. A new Assistant manager shall be chosen from the Freshman class each year to replace the outgoing Head Manager by the managers for the previous year. All managers must be approved by the conductor.[7]

Figure 5.2 – Grilling at the annual Furman Singers fall picnic. Photo courtesy Furman Singers Archives.

Vick relied heavily on student leadership from his first days as conductor of Furman Singers, delegating organizational duties to student managers and many of the social activity planning duties to the officers. Social activities were, in fact, a component of the handbook. Post-examinations retreat to the beach, fall picnic, Christmas party, and spring banquet are mentioned as Furman Singers events, along with less formal activities such as attendance at sporting events, parties, and dances. These activities, though informal, were part of Vick's strategy to create a familial atmosphere in Furman Singers, and he and the officers worked to ensure that new members of the ensemble felt welcomed through them.

The 1982 handbook, in its historical sketch of Furman Singers, gives an account of the comments of an unnamed pastor of a church the Furman Singers visited on tour:

> Following the Singers' concert on a recent tour, the pastor of the church, reflecting on what he had just seen and heard from the Singers, commented that the first thoughts that came to mind were Discipline, Perfection, and Beauty. The purpose of Furman Singers is to perform great music to the best of our ability. We strive to accomplish this goal through a disciplined approach to rehearsals, always doing our best to perfect the intent of the composer and the meaning of the text, and never forgetting that the beautiful sounds we produce and the appropriate image we project visually are but a small part of the Beauty and Perfection of God's creation. It is to Him we sing.[8]

These comments became the basis for the motto of Furman Singers, modified in later years: Discipline, Excellence, Beauty. The appearance of Furman Singers was a focus of the handbooks, as well. Vick stressed that an ensemble's decorum, before, during, and after a performance, can deeply affect an audience's perception of a performance.

Figure 5.3 – The annual Furman Band versus Furman Singers softball game. Photo courtesy Furman Singers Archives.

Vick's relative youth and undeniable enthusiasm precipitated a rapid increase in student interest in Furman Singers. Under Rhame, the audition process had served the purpose of placement in a section rather than an opportunity to ensure that only the best singers participated. Vick continued this policy in the first several years of his tenure. The result was that, by the fall of 1972, Furman Singers numbered more than 150 and would peak at more than 200 students. Indeed, Furman Singers had already reached 200 members by the fall of 1974. In notes directed to the Furman Singers officers Vick detailed three main problems with this level of participation: musical balance, financial strain, and administration.

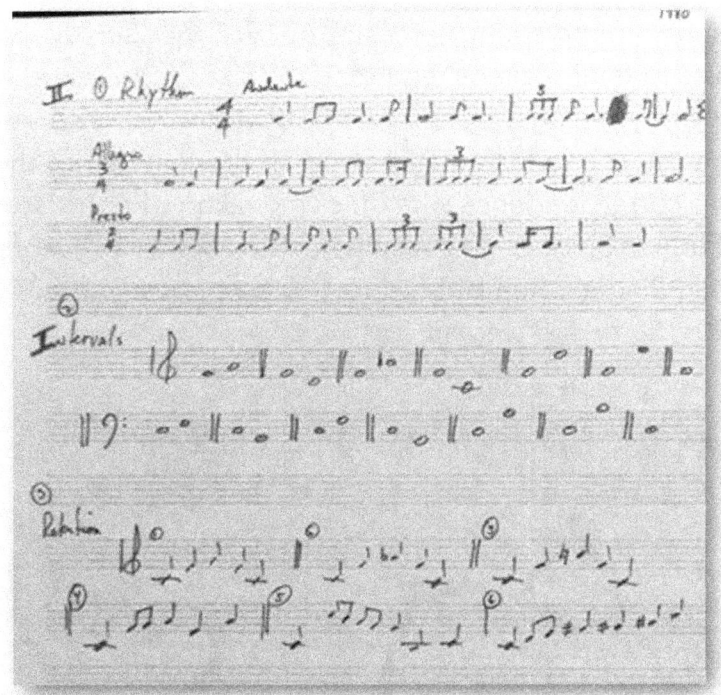

Figure 5.4 – Vick's handwritten audition sheet for the 1980 fall audition. Photo courtesy Furman Singers Archives.

With regard to balance, Furman Singers had a disproportionately large soprano section, with the second soprano part outnumbering other sections and causing the most severe balance issues. In terms of finances, the exceptionally high number of students in Furman Singers meant that Vick had inadequate funds to purchase music and transport the entirety of the ensemble to events. Finally, simple activities such as checking attendance, setting up risers, and preparing for rehearsals through activities such as handing out new music became an unusual burden.[9] Vick announced more stringent auditions for the ensemble and listed three primary qualities he would consider: musical ability, interest and involvement in activities and performances, and reliability in terms of promptness and attendance. In the spring semester of 1975 Vick surveyed Furman Singers as to their feelings regarding the size of the group, the repertoire performed on tour, and several other issues. His files contain notes on the changes in membership in the first half of the 1970s as well as correspondence with officers dealing with the issue of the size of Furman Singers. The result of this work was an eventual drop in Furman Singers membership to 120 by the early 1980s and, by the 1990s, 80 to 100 singers.[10]

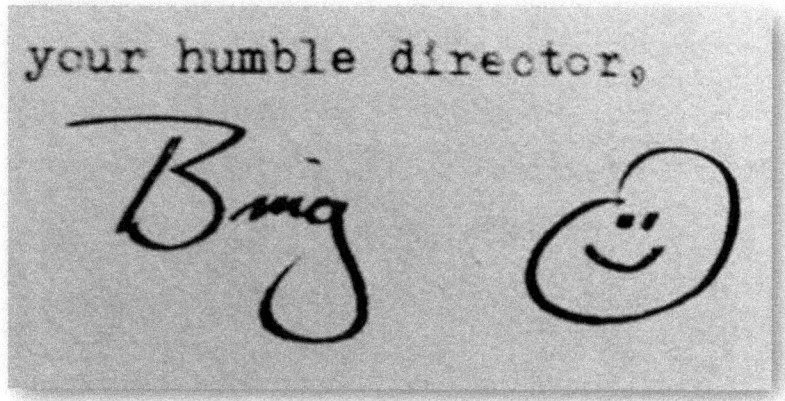

Figure 5.5 – Vick's signature and customary accompanying smiley face. Photo courtesy Furman Singers Archives.

Vick continued to recruit via correspondence even as he worked to decrease Furman Singers membership to a manageable level. Over the summer of 1975 he drafted several hopeful, lengthy letters to his student officers as well, dealing with issues ranging from organizational issues for fall rehearsals to plans for the spring tour.[11] Among the more remarkable features of these letters are his openness to criticism and the enormous trust and emphasis he placed on his student officer structure: "I learn a little more each year about Singers, and I am always ready to hear suggestions about how to improve my working relationships with the group, as well as what will make Singers better and more enjoyable for you members."[12] This trust and appreciation was present in Vick's initial relations with Furman Singers officers as well as in later years with the group, when experience and habit had refined the school year to the point that the ensemble's activities had become second nature.[13] The letters also indicate that Vick and the officers put many hours of work into discussing the social activities that helped make Furman Singers an enduring social network as well as a chorus dedicated to making great music. In large part the mechanics of social organization fell to the president and vice president for implementation: planning and execution of parties, receptions, banquets, interactions with church and school hosts, and a myriad of other functions.

The student leadership structure of Furman Singers was not entirely geared toward the social elements of participation, however. Each year, Vick entrusted one or more students with the role of student conductor. Rather than superficial involvement with the musical activity of the chorus, the student conductors of Furman Singers conducted sectional rehearsals and were responsible for learning all of the repertoire for the year, so as to be able to substitute conduct for Vick in instances of need. The application process involved the submission of a detailed résumé and a conducting audition with Furman Singers on a selection of Vick's choice. Once chosen, in addition to serving as understudies for tour repertoire, student conductors also prepared a single selection each to conduct on tour and at the Furman Singers home concert. These selections were always part of the substantial art music portion of the tour programs, rather than the lighter fare Vick often programmed for the conclusion of the concert. James E. Williams, III, Furman University class of 2000, served as president and student conductor in the 1999 to 2000 school year, and described the pleasure he felt in being entrusted with such weighty musical material at such a young age:

> The piece that I was able to do, the Casals "O Vos Omnes," was a pretty large, 16-part piece that I taught the group. It's not very common that you're able to work with such a fine ensemble at a young age. To have that experience and that opportunity with him as your mentor was pretty remarkable.[14]

Williams also recalled an instance in which Vick offered him the baton during a Furman Singers trip to Europe:

> One of my most significant memories was that, on the last European tour I was able to share… Dr. Vick asked me if there was something on the program I'd like to conduct… and there were so many great things on the program, but I chose the Lauridsen "O Magnum Mysterium" because of the ethereal nature of it and the environment in which we were singing. Him having that kind of confidence in me, turning over something that he had never seen me conduct before, that he felt that I was capable and ready for such a task…That confidence that he had in me was probably the most flattering.[15]

The use of a student conductor was a practice Vick continued throughout his 40 years as director of Furman Singers.

Another key element of the officer structure of Furman Singers was the set of three managers, long known playfully and affectionately by members of the choir as the "managi." These students helped ease the process of handling such a large group of students, in terms of daily mechanics associated with rehearsal, the particular needs of concerts, and especially the ongoing physical and organizational labors of touring domestically and abroad. Student managers were paid a small amount, and the position held the attraction of working closely with Vick, developing friendships with other managers, and a kind of fraternal structure that became a bond of managers past and present. Among many other duties, managers helped with the physical tasks of moving risers and music, pulling and filing music, loading and unloading luggage and concert attire, and organizing student work crews. Vick sent a great deal of correspondence to the managers during the course of a normal school year, and was meticulous in detailing the things Furman Singers needed for concerts in terms of timing and material. The managers themselves drafted letters and instructions to Furman Singers for domestic and European tours, and delighted in exchanging jokes with one another and their peers in the midst of communicating important details.

Figure 5.6 – Furman Singers managers in the spring manager skit, a usual part of the spring banquet and naming of the new sophomore manager. Photo courtesy Furman Singers Archives.

Over years of experience with the management of the student officers of Furman Singers, Vick developed succinct descriptions of the duties for each office and printed these descriptions for the elections that took place each spring term. The president was responsible for the oversight of auditions and the coordination of the partnering program of upper and under classmen in Furman Singers called "Big Brothers, Big Sisters." The president also represented Furman Singers as a student liaison to the music department, presided over officer meetings, assisted with homecoming, and penned a few items of correspondence over the course of the year. The vice president was the social chair and responsible for organizing the reception that came to follow the first rehearsal, the fall picnic at the Vicks' house, and assisting with the spring banquet. The treasurer prepared a fall budget report for approval by the officers, collected dues, and bore the responsibility for sales of recordings, t-shirts, and other small items over the course of the year. The secretary coordinated purchases and changes in the Furman Singers dress, was responsible for attendance, and helped with any photocopying needs. The historian designed the fall t-shirt, created a scrapbook for exhibit at the spring banquet, was responsible for the display table for tour concerts at which recordings were sold, and took pictures of "Big Brothers" and "Big Sisters" with their respective lower classmen partners after the first rehearsal of the year. The managers' duties are outlined above, but Vick also noted that manager positions were not jobs for the sake of money alone: managers were expected to exhibit a strong commitment to Furman Singers, enthusiasm, and leadership. Vick emphasized the importance of maintaining good grades as well.[16]

Vick communicated the planning that took place in the officers' meetings to Furman Singers during rehearsals. Most, if not all, of the themes the officers discussed, with Vick's guidance, became part of his message to the ensemble. This was a usual feature of the first rehearsal each fall, especially, and Vick gave the officers detailed instructions regarding his expectations for their behavior during that rehearsal. He expected the student conductors and accompanist to be impeccably prepared, officers to be highly visible and welcoming, and all to behave with discipline and enthusiasm. In addition to his rules for musicianship printed in the handbook, Vick also became known for a few oft-repeated rules for rehearsal comportment:

> Come to every rehearsal expecting something wonderful to happen. Refining musical sound is an exciting and rewarding activity, if you make it so. Great performances are the result of great rehearsals.[17]

"Early is on time, on time is late, late is unacceptable" was a frequent reminder. The high level of organization and careful planning in the officer group translated into a unified sense of purpose between Vick and the student leadership. Vick's emphasis on clarity and efficiency in his own rehearsal technique was an organic part of the whole.

A Place of Our Own: the Herring Pavilion

Despite great efforts to make Furman Singers a success through organization and planning, for the first 25 years of Vick's time at the helm of the ensemble the group rehearsed in an inadequate and inhospitable space designed for lectures in the sciences. In addition to the cramped conditions caused by high numbers in the 1970s, the managers had to cope with the difficulty of hauling music and other materials to and from McAlister Auditorium and later the adjoining Homozel Mickel Daniel Music Building before and after each rehearsal. By the time of Vick's arrival at Furman University, Furman Singers had been rehearsing in McAlister Auditorium and Townes Lecture Hall for ten years. By January of 1973 it seemed that a change in these less-than-ideal conditions might be possible.

Furman University received a grant of $4,000,000.00 in the fall of 1972 from the Daniel Foundation. The funds were designated for Furman's Music Department to develop "the finest music program in a private college or university in the south."[18] It was, at the time, the largest gift in the history of the college. In addition to allowing for the construction and maintenance of a new music facility, the gift endowed several new professorships and scholarships. As plans for the new building began to take shape, Vick clearly hoped that a rehearsal space for Furman Singers would be part of those plans.[19] Once blueprints for the Homozel Mickel Daniel Music Building were complete, it was clear that this was not to be. The building included new practice rooms, offices and studios, classrooms, a rehearsal space for the band and orchestra, and a handsome recital hall, but no rehearsal space suitable for Furman Singers. It would be almost 20 years before Furman Singers would have facilities adequate for the needs of the ensemble.

Figure 5.7 – Vick in rehearsal in Townes Lecture Hall.
Photo courtesy Furman Singers Archives.

By the early 1990s the alumni of Furman Singers numbered in the thousands, and Dave Vassy, Furman University class of 1974 and a former manager, realized that great potential existed in those numbers for a gift of real significance as Furman Singers approached its fiftieth anniversary year. Vassy also recognized that another milestone was approaching: Vick's 25th year as director of Furman Singers. In a conversation with Vick at the Furman Singers reunion in Charleston in 1993, Vassy asked if there were anything in particular Vick needed for Furman Singers. Vick, half in jest, suggested that what Furman Singers really needed was a new rehearsal space. Vassy's faith in the enthusiasm and sheer numbers of alumni interested in Furman Singers would be sufficient for such an undertaking, however, and he began to lay the groundwork for a major fundraising project.[20]

Vassy's vision for the project included roughly equal donations from Furman Singers alumni. He met with Don Lineback of Furman University's development office, who quickly disabused Vassy of that notion. Lineback explained that fundraising of this magnitude typically involved a sizeable donation by a single donor, some lesser donations, and then the small donations on which Vassy thought Furman Singers might rely would eventually account for a small minority of the total funds needed. Lineback, impressed with the enthusiasm and determination of Vassy and others, set to work in assisting the Furman Singers alumni.

Gordon Herring, Furman University class of 1965 and former Furman Singers manager, and his wife Sarah, Furman University class of 1966, are proud to be alumni of the chorus. Gordon Herring, after earning an M.B.A. from the University of Virginia and serving in the United States Army for three years, had joined TeleCable Corporation as director of research. Over his 19 years of employment with TeleCable, Herring eventually became executive vice president, retiring after the company's sale. He was awarded an honorary doctor of laws degree from Furman University in 1991 and was serving as a trustee when Vassy first approached the Furman University Development Office. The Herrings would have been quite well known to the administration and to Don Lineback.

Lineback visited with the Herrings and, after Lineback explained the initiative, the Herrings were convinced of the worthiness of the cause. Furman University officials announced the Herrings' donation of $1.25 million on Monday, September 18, 1995.[21] This large sum served to drive the campaign forward to its eventual goal of $2.8 million. The building would be named the Nan Trammell Herring Music Pavilion in honor of Gordon Herring's mother, who had graduated from Furman University in 1929 and was responsible for the introduction to the campus of the traditional serenade, "Brown Eyes," as discussed in Chapter 3. In order to encourage the remaining necessary donations, the Development Office offered naming opportunities for a variety of gift levels, including the rehearsal hall, library, computer lab, and conference room. The rehearsal hall for Furman Singers was named the Elizabeth Stone Harper Recital Hall in honor of Lib Harper, an alumna of the Greenville Woman's College. The groundbreaking for the building took place in the fall of 1996, one year after the announcement of the Herrings' gift.

The path to that ceremony involved a great deal of work on the part of the Furman Singers alumni. In addition to the work on the part of the Development Office, these alumni made phone calls and visits to hundreds of potential donors to the project, eventually involving more than 400 Furman Singers. Their efforts ensured that the pavilion would become the first project on Furman University's campus to be completely funded and endowed before occupancy. The Greenville-based architectural firm Craig, Gaulden, and Davis designed the pavilion. Furman Singers began rehearsals in the facility in the fall of 1997 and, after little more than a year of construction, the building was dedicated on March 5, 1998 with a concert by the ensemble. After more than 50 years, Furman Singers had a dedicated rehearsal space.

Figure 5.8 – The exterior of the Nan Trammell Herring Music Pavilion.

The Last Month of the Year, the First Concert

Organizational challenges and the beginnings of ensemble cohesion were the immediate concerns of the beginning of each year, and Furman Singers certainly had musical obligations before December of each year. The first major concert of the fall, however, was the *Messiah* performance that had been so successful during DuPre Rhame's tenure. Vick, fresh from graduate school and perhaps experiencing some of the same doubts Jerry Langenkamp had expressed about the annual *Messiah* performance, decided to make substantial changes to the program in his first year. His most recent experience of the work had been a Northwestern University performance in which the conductor went to great lengths to attempt an approximation of Handel's ensemble, both in terms of size and in terms of performance practice. Rhame preferred a large chorus and believed that only professional soloists could do the work justice. Vick wanted to bring this type of experience to Furman University, which meant a dramatic paring down of the orchestra and chorus. Vick also wanted to use student soloists rather than professionals from outside the community, faculty members, or other adults. The two agreed to disagree and, in the performance, Vick managed to implement both changes successfully, using only current Furman University students rather than keeping the chorus open to Furman University alumni and members of local churches. In order to achieve the nimbleness of the smaller ensemble he had in mind, he divided the singers into a *ripieno* chorus and a *concertino* chorus. He also found that undergraduate soloists performed quite well.

One can easily imagine the kind of reaction the Greenville community members might have had to changes of this sort to a longstanding tradition. Vick handled the changes as diplomatically as possible, noting in the performance program that "in 1859, when the British observed the centenary of Handel's death, the *Messiah* orchestra numbered 460 players with a chorus of 2,700," but also pointing out that "Handel's...score indicates an orchestra of 40 players at most, and a chorus of comparable size."[22] Thomas Mosely's article in *The Greenville News* did not help Vick's case with the Greenville Community, however, as it emphasized the notion that the 1970 performance would return Handel's masterwork to its "correct" proportions with its headline "*Messiah* Returns to Handel Tradition at FU Sunday."[23] The newspaper reported the size of the chorus, which was still quite large, at 200 voices, with 40 in the *concertino* chorus and a 36 piece orchestra. Both Vick and Furman

Singers alumna Lloyd Linney recalled that Rhame enjoyed joking with Vick about the size of the chorus for years afterward. The performance was broadcast on more than 180 radio stations in 48 states, including Alaska and Hawaii. The 1971 performance would be broadcast on a similarly large number of stations, but added *The Christmas Story* by Ron Nelson to the program, the beginnings of a broadening in the Christmas repertoire and a movement away from yearly performances of *Messiah*. In 1972 the chorus was substantially larger, numbering 300, and the popularity of the performance had not suffered: it was once again broadcast over most of the United States. The first half of the program was devoted to a performance of Benjamin Britten's *A Ceremony of Carols*, conducted by Vick, while Dan Boda conducted the *Messiah* portion of the program. In the following years the ensemble conductors began to rotate the responsibility of conducting the Christmas oratorio performance, and occasionally programs excluded *Messiah* entirely. In 1975 DuPre Rhame returned to the podium to conduct the *Messiah* performance. The soloists were, appropriately, faculty members, including Vick as tenor soloist. An enthusiastic audience greeted Rhame and the performance was well received.

Over the next 35 years the annual Christmas concert became freer in its structure and the various conductors exercised greater liberty in their programming. *Messiah* performances continued with some regularity, but Vick, Boda, and others programmed other masterworks, as well. The *Dona Nobis Pacem* and *Hodie* of Ralph Vaughan Williams, *Gloria* of Francis Poulenc, *Magnificat, Cantata Number 140, Christmas Oratorio* of J.S. Bach, *Gloria* of Antonio Vivaldi, and *Une Cantate de Noel* of Arthur Honegger featured on the programs in addition to *The Christmas Story* and *Ceremony of Carols* mentioned above. Christmas performances continued to represent collaborations between the entirety of the music department and Furman Singers continued to provide the core of the vocal ensemble.

Furman Singers and University Chorus

When Bingham Vick, Jr. came to Furman University, Milburn Price was still the director of the Concert Choir. This meant that Furman University, a school of less than 3,000 students, had two touring choruses, each relatively large. Though the two conductors remained friendly both personally and professionally, the parallel goals of the two ensembles created a difficult situation in the fall, as both Vick and Price competed for much of the same student talent. After the fall audition process, however, the two conductors collaborated on many of the largest music department events during the remainder of the year, including the Christmas concert and the spring oratorio, which took the place of the spring opera in the first year of Rhame's retirement.

Both Vick and Price found the situation strange and discussed possible solutions almost annually. Price proposed the possibility of combining the two ensembles and alternating the directorship between the two of them, but both Vick and Price felt very strongly about the identity of the Concert Choir and Furman Singers. Price's emphasis tended toward church music, whereas Furman Singers filled a more general musical role and in Vick's view should maintain its identity for the sake of its significantly longer history.[24] In the end it was Milburn Price who settled the situation.

Conservative members of the Southern Baptist Convention began to place political pressure on the various institutions of the convention in the late 1970s and early 1980s. Vick recalled that Price, who had the respect of conservatives in the convention because of his credentials as a high-caliber church musician, felt that he could fill the much-needed role of conciliator between those in the convention, such as Vick, who wished to maintain high standards of musicianship and those who wished to place greater emphasis on evangelical goals, by taking the position of dean of the School of Music at the Southern Baptist Theological Seminary. Price left Furman University at the end of the 1980 to 1981 school year.

Price's departure marked the opportunity to restructure the choral program at Furman University, and a letter to Vick from John Crabtree, Vice President of Student Affairs, dated July 8, 1981, indicates that the question of how best to handle merging the two ensembles had been on the minds of the administration for some time. The tone of the letter also indicates that the issue of integrating the two ensembles involved interests of more parties than Price and Vick, as Price was no longer part of the discussion: "It is quite impossible to satisfy everyone's wishes as regards a name for the group, repertory, emphases, student leadership, etc. Trying to make everyone happy will result in decisions that make no one happy."[25] Crabtree suggested that the two ensembles combine into a single touring group for the 1981 to 1982 school year. He further suggested that the ensemble be called Furman Singers. Sensitive to the 20-year history of Concert Choir, Crabtree suggested that promotional materials for the fall carefully explain the combination of the two groups and that Vick proceed with caution regarding auditions for the fall and former Concert Choir members. As there was little to no overlap between the two choruses, Crabtree encouraged Vick to allow the opportunity for Concert Choir students to fill student leadership roles in Furman Singers. Finally, Crabtree urged Vick to be sensitive to hurt feelings that might arise through the use of language such as "abolished" and "taken over."

The integration of the two groups seems to have been accomplished with little trouble.[26] In order to absorb the large number of students who wished to participate in an ensemble without once again overloading Furman Singers, the music department created a new ensemble, the University Chorus, for students who were not part of Furman Singers. In the fall of 1981, just as Crabtree had suggested, the pamphlet detailing the singing opportunities at Furman University carefully laid out the mission and audition policies of Furman Singers. It also made clear that Furman Singers membership would be limited to 100 voices, that this would mean a very limited number of spots for new singers, and that the touring ensemble would be limited to 75 voices by another, separate audition later in the year, a practice that continued for the remainder of Vick's tenure. University Chorus became an ensemble open to any student interested in singing and held auditions for the sole purpose of placing students in the appropriate section according to voice type. Without Price on the faculty, Vick was forced to take charge of the new ensemble and initially conducted Furman Singers, Furman Chamber Singers, and the University Chorus. Vick soon realized that this arrangement would be unsustainable given his other responsibilities at the university, as director of a church choir, and the Greenville Chorale, a community ensemble. Ramon Kyser, professor of voice, became the director for the 1984 to 1985 school year. In 1985 Furman University hired Carl Beard to conduct the University Chorus.

Chamber and Small Ensembles Associated with Furman Singers
Jerry Langenkamp's chamber ensemble, comprised of and operating within Furman Singers, dissolved on Rhame's retirement and Langenkamp's move to Kansas. Vick enjoyed the dynamics of a

small, chamber ensemble as compared with the large and rapidly growing numbers in Furman Singers, and formed the Furman Chamber Singers in his second full year on faculty at Furman University. Vick's intentions included offering the very best musicians in Furman Singers another creative outlet, a chance to perform chamber music of the highest quality, and providing greater depth and range to the programming for Furman Singers annual spring tour. The group was comprised of 16 to 20 singers. Furman Chamber Singers also performed separately from Furman Singers, even in its earliest days of existence, presenting a far more mobile musical force than its larger parent ensemble.

Repertoire for the first performances in the fall of 1971 included Jean Berger's "Five Quotations," Paul Hindemith's "Six Chansons," a Ward Swingle arrangement of a canon by J.S. Bach as a transitional selection, and two arrangements of Burt Bacharach hits "Promises, Promises" and "What the World Needs Now." This was reflective of Vick's programming style with Furman Singers, discussed in greater depth in Chapter 6, and became a template for most Furman Chamber Singers concerts with Vick over the next 30 years. Furman Chamber Singers often collaborated with other small ensembles in Furman University's music department, including Robert Chesebro, a professor on the wind faculty, and the Woodwind Ensemble, Thomas Joiner, conductor of the Furman University Symphony Orchestra, and the Chamber Philharmonic Society, and Dan Ellis, conductor of the Furman Band, and the Chamber Jazz Ensemble. Broadly, programs often began with music from the Renaissance, Baroque, Classical, or Romantic periods of western music history, included selections from contemporary trends in art music, and then moved to selections of popular music, and especially music of a humorous nature. Vick's unique affinity for humor in music would become a theme of his career with Furman Chamber Singers, and he often programmed the music of composers such as William Bergsma, Ward Swingle, and Peter Schickele, a composer who is better known by his *nom de plume* P.D.Q. Bach. The latter became a particular favorite, with several concerts exclusively devoted to his music. Schickele's music held particular interest for Vick, who earned his Ph.D. in historical studies, because of Schickele's ability to satirize the foibles of musicologists and the contemporary trend toward historically informed efforts at authenticity in performance.[27] The first concert by Furman Chamber Singers entirely comprised of music by P.D.Q. Bach took place on May 17, 1977, at 8:13pm in the recently constructed Daniel Recital Hall. Selections included "The Stoned Guest," "The Art of the Ground Round," "Two Madrigals from 'The Triumph of Thusnelda,'" and "The Seasonings." Vick included several musicians playing strings, wind, brass, and percussion on the program, choreographed and staged much of the music, and costumed himself and the singers. He also penned extensive, satirical program notes.[28]

The success of the concert was such that it became a biennial event. For other performances Vick continued to program representative works from the entire scope of western art music and collaborate with chamber ensembles from Furman University's music department. In 1993 Vick began a correspondence with Peter Schickele related to a Furman Chamber Singers performance of Schickele's "Two Hearts, Four Lips, Three Little Words."[29] In the letters, Vick and Schickele discuss "Two Hearts," which Furman Chamber Singers had commissioned, as well as the possibility of a workshop involving Schickele to take place in the spring of 1995. Schickele and Vick also discuss program notes for "Two Hearts," which Schickele eventually provided:

Paris Mountain, in Greenville, South Carolina, would seem to be an unlikely place to discover an original music manuscript by any composer, much less an 18th century German composer who, as far as we know, never visited the New World. And it is.[30]

Figure 5.9 – Peter Schickele in rehearsal with the Furman Symphony Orchestra. Photo courtesy Furman Singers Archives.

Schickele goes on to describe his "discovery" of the work, a conceit he frequently employed for humorous effect, and signs his name "Professor Peter Schickele, Chairman, Department of Musical Pathology, University of Southern North Dakota at Hoople."

Vick and Schickele continued frequent communications over the course of the next two years, culminating in the workshop at Furman University the pair had discussed in 1993. Vick worked closely with Martha Vaughn, part of the university's administration, in planning the details of the visit and traveled to New York City in order to meet with Schickele in person and discuss particulars.

Plans included a visit to the Fine Arts school in Greenville, work with Mark Kilstofte, professor of composition, his theory and composition classes, and rehearsals with Furman Chamber Singers, Furman Singers, and Furman Symphony Orchestra. Vick's projected budget for the week amounted to $31,884 in expenses and $36,650 in income, principally from ticket sales, but also from a corporate sponsorship from AT&T. The expenses included Schickele's $15,000 fee, licensing for the music, production costs, lodging, print materials, and publicity. *The Greenville News* ran coverage of Schickele's visit, including an extensive article outlining the week's visit and performances open to the public.[31] Furman University President David Shi and his wife Susan hosted the composer, Bingham and Judy Vick, and other guests at White Oaks, the home of Furman University's president, following the concert. Reception of the concert was positive and Vick maintained professional communication with Schickele afterward.

For most of the 30 years Vick conducted Furman Chamber Singers, the ensemble was closely connected with Furman Singers through its complete overlap in membership and the confinement of its independent concerts to Furman University's campus and the Greenville community. In 1999, however, Vick utilized Furman Chamber Choir, which had been renamed in 1997, as a demonstration choir at an interest session at the 1999 National Convention of the American Choral Directors Association. Vick entitled the session "Humor in Choral Music."[32] In addition to Vick's notes regarding the general value of laughter in the concert setting and the history of humor in art music, Furman Chamber Choir performed several selections in a variety of styles, including P.D.Q. Bach's "Oedipus Tex," Franz Joseph Haydn's "An Admonition," William Bergsma's "Riddle Me This," Norman Luboff's "Much Ado About Nothings," Paul Sjolund's "Love Lost," John Rutter's "Banquet Fugue," and

Ward Swingle's "Music History 101." The session took place in a large ballroom and the Furman Chamber Choir performed to a full house. Vick repeated the performance on Furman University's campus. Later that year, the spring concert of 1999 returned to the staples of Furman Chamber Choir's repertoire. The spring concert would be Vick's last concert as director of the ensemble.

William Thomas replaced Carl Beard as conductor of the University Chorus. Thomas was, at that time, the director of music at the First Baptist Church of Greenville. Furman University's administration later hired Thomas to work as a full time faculty member, creating a second chamber ensemble for Thomas called the Furman Chamber Choir. Thomas conducted Chamber Choir with the mission of performing sacred music in churches around the region. Unlike the Concert Choir, no conflict existed between Furman Chamber Singers and the new Furman Chamber Choir in terms of rehearsal time. This meant, in effect, that a significant overlap existed between the membership in Chamber Choir and Chamber Singers. Compounding the problem of personnel overlap was the creation of a significant scholarship award associated with membership in Chamber Choir. This situation began to create tension between the conductors of the two ensembles and the department's voice faculty members, who were well aware of the strain on their students' time and vocal health. In April of 1995 Thomas and Vick exchanged emails regarding possible solutions to the problem and, after a conversation in early May, mutually agreed to enact a solution that echoed Milburn Price's proposals for the dilemma that had faced Furman Singers and the Concert Choir: the ensembles would be combined and Vick and Thomas would alternate as conductors every other year. This arrangement lasted until 2000. Thomas was by then chair of the music department, a position that carries great authority over the department's scholarship funds and ensemble structure, among other things. At the end of that year, acting as chairman of the department, Thomas made the decision that Chamber Choir would become his responsibility alone. Vick appealed Thomas's decision to Furman University's administration to no avail.[33]

In addition to the Furman Chamber Singers, Furman Singers spawned three other ensembles. Two of those ensembles, the Mosquitoes and Honeybees, focused on traditional barbershop literature. The third, the Furman Folk Ensemble, focused on American folksong repertoire. Vick and three students, Dave Vassy, Ty Talton, and George Eison, founded the Mosquitoes in the fall of 1971 as an informal venture, with only one song in their repertoire, from which they took their name. The quartet proved popular among the students. Vick, satisfied that their sound was worthy of programming on concerts with Furman Singers as part of the group's more lighthearted fare, included the Mosquitoes on tour and at home concerts. Vick also took the Mosquitoes to various civic functions around Greenville when he needed an especially small ensemble for a given function. Vick sang as part of the quartet for his entire tenure at Furman University.

In 1985 four of Vick's sopranos and altos, Julia Wilson, Paige Overton, Kelley Batson, and Melissa Sexton, came to Vick and proposed a quartet of sopranos and altos. In subsequent years the story would feature in stage introductions of the group with the unison exclamation, "We demand equal time!" Vick agreed to the students' proposal, and the Honeybees became part of the tour presence of Furman Singers. Joe Liles' eight-part partner song, "Fun in Just One Lifetime" was a staple of the quartets' repertoire. Another small group, the Furman Folk Ensemble, performed for a short time as part of Furman Singers. Jane Swindler, Mark Powers, and Allan Fulmer founded the group in 1975. The trio had performed together as part of the First Baptist Church of Columbia. They composed and performed their own music alongside the Mosquitoes and Honeybees on tour and at home concerts.

Figure 5.10 – Mosquitoes and Honeybees in concert.
Photo courtesy Furman Singers Archives.

Furman Singers on Tour

Furman Singers toured throughout DuPre Rhame's tenure. During Vick's tenure tour was as important if not more important. Planning for tour certainly occupied much of Vick's time and attention. In addition to carefully selecting tour repertoire, planning involved several administrative elements, including extensive correspondence with prospective hosts, churches, and schools, budget planning and reconciliation of actual expenses and income with projected expenses and income, and management of the extensive logistical issues attendant to tour. The Furman Singers Archives contain reams of correspondence related to tour. Vick's first year serves as a representative sample of the kind of work involved in managing an educationally oriented ensemble's interests balanced against the interests of churches and universities with mutual ties to the Southern Baptist Convention. In most cases Vick maintained that balance without incident. In a few, rare cases, Vick defended his decisions against the complaints of music ministers and parishioners who were, understandably, more interested in the needs of the church than the needs of the university students. Each set of letters provides a unique window into the 1970 to 1971 school year for Furman Singers.

In November of 1970, Vick wrote the Reverend James Thompson, the senior minister at the First Baptist Church of Vero Beach, inquiring as to whether the church might be willing to host Furman Singers for a concert and an overnight stay in the spring of 1971. Thompson answered in the affirmative, but Vick also received a letter from Larry Henry, minister of music, indicating a preference that all of the music Furman Singers performed be "church music." Henry assured Vick that this did not imply that the music should be traditional, only that it should be sacred. Vick addressed the issue of secular versus sacred repertoire and performance location with many of the churches he contacted, at times requesting a separate time for the secular portion of the concert.[34]

Vick worked very hard to arrange a performance at his alma mater, Stetson University. His first letters were to Paul Langston, dean of the school of music at Stetson. Vick was most interested in whether or not Stetson would be touring, hopeful that, in planning a trip to Florida, he would not find himself competing for venues and an audience with another touring choir with a very similar profile. Vick reported that his first weeks at Furman University had exceeded his expectations and he looked forward to touring Florida with his ensemble. Langston replied that the Stetson choir, under the direction of Vick's mentor, Harold M. Giffin, would not be touring that spring and that Stetson University would be very happy to host the Furman Singers. Happy to have the opportunity to return to familiar ground, Vick continued with plans to visit the school, working closely with W. Michael Chertok of Stetson University's Development Department.[35]

In a series of letters exchanged with Lloyd Landrum, minister of music at Vineville Baptist Church in Macon, Georgia, Vick reported that his first performance of Handel's *Messiah* had gone well: "My tempi and 'interpretation' were both rather different from the previous 35 years with Mr. Rhame, but everyone seems to have survived, so I guess all is well."³⁶ Vick also reported that, for their visit to Vineville, Furman Singers would perform in formal outfits and requested that the ensemble be permitted to use the church's robes, as they would only be singing in church services for two performances and wished to avoid carrying the robes, if possible. Edwin S. Irey, minister of music at the First Baptist Church of Orlando, Florida, encouraged Vick to allow the students to wear their formal attire for the Sunday morning worship service, noting, "Our people are used to having things done in good taste and style."³⁷ In this and several other instances Vick discusses the possibility of the collection of a "free will offering," or an informal collection of funds in the middle of the concerts given at churches. Vick cited a limited budget, and requested that churches provide an evening meal before the concerts and breakfast the next morning, as well.³⁸

Enthusiastic audiences greeted Furman Singers, and Vick received several letters of congratulations, thanks, support, and encouragement from those he had contacted in the fall of 1970. Dean Paul Langston of Stetson University wrote, "It is a source of pride for all of us to see the fine work that you are doing."³⁹ Landrum wrote to Vick as well "Our people thoroughly enjoyed hearing the singers and keeping them in our homes. You have done an outstanding job."⁴⁰ Edward S. French wrote that "people were unanimous in their enthusiasm and appreciation" after the Furman Singers performance at Haver Hill Baptist Church in West Palm Beach, Florida.⁴¹ Furman Singers received a telegram from DuPre Rhame at a stop in Orlando, Florida: "My love and best wishes to each of you. Have a wonderful tour and hurry back home."⁴² Vick believed that having a small taste of spring vacation was an important element of tour, and took the Furman Singers to Cypress Gardens in Winter Haven, Florida, as part of that trip.

Many of the themes that emerged during Vick's first year planning tour for Furman Singers would resurface in the following years. Vick learned from his first year's planning that many organizations' leadership, whether serving churches or not, valued a clear understanding of the nature of the repertoire of Furman Singers. He made a point of mentioning the divide between the sacred and secular portions of the program in his initial letter of introduction. Some organizations responded very favorably to the variety of music that was part of the Furman Singers concerts. Troupe Harris, Concert Chairman of the Music Society of Washington, Georgia and liaison between Vick and that group, wrote that he felt "the pop tunes and Bacharach songs on the program…will increase…appreciation of the entire program."[43] Churches were more sensitive to the divide in the repertoire, particularly with regard to the performance venue. R.D. Roberts, minister of music at Shandon Baptist Church, in Columbia, South Carolina, wrote that his congregation would "prefer an all-sacred concert for the sanctuary, and although we would enjoy the secular entertainment afterwards, perhaps we had better forego that in the interest of time and getting you to your places of lodging at a reasonable hour."[44]

As Furman University's most fertile recruiting territory, most tours involved visits to Georgia, Florida, and the Carolinas, though Vick also planned tours that ventured further afield than those of his predecessor, taking Furman Singers out of the southeast on multiple occasions. In the spring of 1973 Vick took Furman Singers to visit another familiar location, the city of Chicago. Bruce Schoonmaker, a member of the voice faculty at Furman University, was a student of Vick's on that 1973 visit. Schoonmaker remembers the joint concert with Northwestern University's Chapel Choir as a particularly satisfying musical moment of that year's tour.[45] The 1974 spring tour included another personal detour, this time to Pritchard Memorial Baptist Church, the church Vick attended as a child and young adult. Furman Singers also participated in the American Choral Directors Association Southern Regional Convention that year and were awarded a key to the city of Chattanooga, Tennessee. Mayor

Robert Kirk Walker named them "Ambassadors of Good Will."[46] In 1975 the ensemble traveled to New Orleans.

Vick and the student officers worked hard to make the Furman Singers spring trip of 1976 exceptional, as it included stops in Washington D.C. in the midst of the United States' bicentennial celebrations.[47] Vick and Marilyn D. Schneider, a student in Furman Singers, penned a series of letters to South Carolina Congressman James R. Mann, United States Senators Strom Thurmond and Ernest F. Hollings, and President Gerald Ford asking for assistance with arrangements for visiting the capitol, touring the White House, and securing performance opportunities.[48] Furman Singers toured the capitol and the White House as part of their trip. New in the 1975 to 1976 correspondence is Vick's request for a guarantee of $150 from each of the churches Furman Singers visited on tour.

Letters from Furman University alumni and Furman Singers alumni to Vick and to Furman University's administration indicate that the ensemble was warmly received on each of its tours in the 1970s and beyond. Among the few criticisms repeatedly offered to Vick over his many years of touring was the complaint that pieces in languages other than English failed to communicate with the audience. Some of these criticisms were more jocular than others. Joe Short, Furman University class of 1951, wrote to Vick on March 12, 1975:

> In last night's concert your group was sensational! ...You engulfed the audience with aesthetically uplifting music and it was almost breathtaking. (Latin and German are beyond my comprehension, so I missed the lyrical message, but the musical harmony came through in all of its splendor.) With tongue in cheek – I believe it was in your Frostiana number that Robert Frost admonishes, "use words that we can comprehend."[49]

W. Richard Wynn, pastor of the Seminole Baptist Church of Tallahassee, Florida, was not so kind, and copied his letter to Dr. John Johns, Furman University's President:

> [Furman Singers] did not communicate with our congregation. They sang all but three selections in German and Latin…I believe that Furman University is committed to proclaiming the Gospel to all men, just as our church is. I would suggest that you let this great choir share their excellent ability and training in a way that most people can share in their message.[50]

Vick's response to Jacques M. Kearns, minister of music at the First Baptist Church of Augusta, Georgia, after receiving a cautionary letter regarding repertoire, offered a defense of his programming philosophy, stating that, through his programming, he hoped to provide "something for everyone" at the concerts of Furman Singers, including music that represented all historical periods and styles. With regard to anthems typically performed by church choir, Vick noted that he avoided that repertoire because of the frequency of its performance in the churches Furman Singers visited on tour as well as the likelihood that students would have the opportunity to perform that literature elsewhere.[51] Though Vick continued to receive occasional complaints regarding music selections in languages other than English, he nevertheless continued to program music he believed to be of value to performer and audience alike.

Realizing the value of tour in terms of its relationship with prospective students as well as alumni, Furman University partially funded the Furman Singers spring trip, but Vick regularly struggled with budgetary restrictions.[52] To help maintain the good standing of Furman Singers with the university's administration, Vick made a point of inviting key individuals to the concerts at the conclusion of tour. Vick included in those invitations copies of letters he received from grateful alumni, host families, and church and school liaisons.[53] In a 1989 letter to Furman University Vice President John Crabtree and Charlotte Smith, chair of the music department, Vick offered a forceful defense of the Furman Singers tour and its costs:

> The Furman Singers have proven to be one of Furman's finest ambassadors over the years, showing churches (congregations) and individuals (through the budget-demanded home stays each evening) exactly what kind of student and quality institution we represent…Our tour is important for Furman because of the PR function it fulfills. It is important educationally and musically for us to maintain a high-quality choral ensemble. It is important for the students (who give up their spring break vacation) to have an enjoyable experience on this tour.[54]

Despite occasional disagreements over the tour budget, Crabtree and Smith were strong advocates for Furman Singers.

Charlotte Smith was an early mentor to Vick, in fact. Vick valued Smith's experienced feedback and friendship immensely. After each year's spring tour Furman Singers presented a concert of the repertoire performed on tour. Smith offered Vick her praise and criticism after each concert. These comments ranged from high praise to frank criticism and sometimes included elements of both. Of the 1975 performance of Johannes Brahms' "O Savior, Rend the Heavens on High," for example, she wrote that the performance was "extremely well-phrased, colorful, beautiful – I wearied a bit toward the end." She also included a complaint regarding a young woman's dress. Of the 1980 performance she noted the consistency of the choir's resonance, the quality of its diction, and the quick and orderly changes in formation that accompanied two of the works. She succinctly summarized her opinion of the contemporary popular music: "Fun music was fun."[55] Her comments were often teasing of Vick, and she began to call him a "geriatric marvel" well before he had reached 50 years of age. Her final postscript to her criticism, written after the 1988 spring concert, reflects her fondness and kind support for Vick:

> The geriatric marvel on the podium, a softening of the brain notwithstanding, shows no evidence of the decline of physical potency in such expected symptoms as stiffening of the joints, faltering of the step and creaking of the bones. Whether blessing or threat, the assumption that he will conduct many more years of excellent Singers concerts is grounded in the convincing evidence seen and heard in [this] concert; but there will not, cannot be a concert more beautiful in tone and musicality, in sheer nurturing of the highest aesthetic senses, than the March 10, 1988 concert.[56]

Vick conducted 22 more concerts, most of which followed on the heels of a busy touring season. Charlotte Smith's superlative comment notwithstanding, Furman Singers continued to perform to the great appreciation of the Greenville community each spring.

The Spring Oratorio Concert

DuPre Rhame's predilection for opera and operetta helped determine the focus of Furman University's music department each spring following the tours of Furman Singers. After his retirement, the music department shifted focus from staged productions to major works, which included secular and sacred oratorio, Masses, and canticles. On rare occasions these spring presentations were comprised of many smaller works on a theme or by a single composer, but the event came to be called the "spring oratorio" regardless. The performances were collaborations between much of the music faculty, and Vick became part of a rotating schedule of conductors that involved the Furman Band, Furman Symphony Orchestra, Furman Singers, and Furman Chamber Choir. Through these performances Furman University students gained the opportunity to hear and perform masterworks ranging from J.S. Bach's *Mass in B Minor* to Carl Orff's *Carmina Burana*. Furman Singers provided the core of the vocal ensemble for each performance, singing alongside members of the various other choral ensembles of the school.

Daniel Boda conducted the first of these performances, *A German Requiem* by Johannes Brahms. In this instance and most others over the course of the next 40 years, students provided the orchestra, chorus, and solos. Gail Graham, now Gail Schoonmaker, voice faculty member at Furman University and wife of Bruce Schoonmaker, also on the voice faculty, sang the soprano solos in the work. Lindsay O'Rear sang the baritone solos, and Jim Hawkins served as his understudy. Vick prepared both Furman Singers and Concert Choir for the performance. The following year the music department presented a series of four concerts encompassing a wide variety of British music in honor of the one hundredth anniversary of the birth of Ralph Vaughan Williams. The first three concerts presented smaller form works such as piano solos, airs, organ works, part songs, and pieces for wind band. Composers represented included Henry Purcell, G.F. Handel, Edward Elgar, and others. The fourth concert presented symphonic works performed by the Furman Symphony Orchestra with Daniel Boda conducting and Ralph Vaughan Williams' *Dona Nobis Pacem* with Vick conducting.

In the spring of 1974 Furman Singers and the Furman Concert Choir collaborated with the Greenville Symphony Orchestra under the direction of Peter Rickett. The first half of the program consisted of a work for guitar and orchestra by Joaquin Rodrigo while the second half was a joint presentation of Carl Orff's *Carmina Burana*. Milburn Price and Vick prepared the choirs separately and Vick served as the tenor soloist. It is notable that, though situated on the outskirts of the city in 1974, the Greenville Symphony Orchestra's performances took place in Furman University's McAlister Auditorium, the most suitable location in the Greenville vicinity. The university would collaborate with the Greenville Symphony Orchestra again in 1976, this time in a performance of Gustav Mahler's *Symphony No. 2 in C minor*. In 1975 the music department presented a single work, this time selecting W.A. Mozart's *Requiem*. Daniel Boda conducted the work.

In the spring of 1982 Bingham Vick, Jr. found that he had total creative control of the choral ensembles at Furman University. That spring, rather than present a single major work, Vick elected to conduct Furman Singers and the Furman University Chorus in collaboration the Furman Brass Ensemble in a variety of works, including Richard Peek's *Stations on the Road to Freedom,* Ralph Vaughan Williams' *Mass in G Minor,* Halsey Stevens' *Te Deum,* and Ralph Vaughan Williams' *O Clap Your Hands*. Vick was able to program such an extensive program by dividing the Furman Singers and Furman University Chorus for some works and combining them for others.

In 1985 Furman Singers performed J.S. Bach's *Mass in B Minor*, the first performance of the work on Furman University's campus. Furman Singers combined with the Furman University Chorus and Furman Symphony Orchestra to create an ensemble that numbered more than 170. Vick conducted the work. His next opportunity to conduct came with the spring performance of Franz Josef Haydn's *The Creation* in 1988. Vick also conducted the music department's second presentation of Carol Orff's *Carmina Burana* in 1990, the school's first performance independent of the Greenville Symphony

Orchestra. In letters to Furman Singers and letters of thanks to participants in the concert, Vick was particularly ebullient:

> *Carmina Burana* was a true "peak experience"! Many have told me that your performance was the most enjoyable and exciting they had ever heard or been a part of. I had a great time working on it with you and bringing it to the audience in such an exuberant way! WAFNA! (that can also mean "congratulations"!)[57]

Among the works presented in subsequent years by Furman Singers and the Furman University music department were Felix Mendelssohn's *Elijah*, Giacomo Puccini's *Messa di Gloria*, Maurice Duruflé's *Requiem*, Leonard Bernstein's *Chichester Psalms*, Giuseppe Verdi's *Quattro Pezzi Sacri*, Franz Joseph Haydn's *Te Deum*, Arthur Honegger's *King David*, and Ralph Vaughan Williams' *A Sea Symphony*.

Notable Performances

In addition to the performances that constituted the routine of the school year, Furman Singers frequently performed for special occasions on campus and elsewhere. Furman Singers often performed for the South Carolina Baptist Convention as part of the university's efforts to uphold positive relations with the convention. Educational groups and events affiliated with church music often called on the chorus to feature in performances around the state, including performances for the South Carolina Music Teachers Association, Kiwanis Club events, and the Furman University Church Music Conference. Early in the 1970s Furman Singers collaborated with the Greenville Symphony Orchestra, the Atlanta Symphony Orchestra, and its conductor Robert Shaw. This collaboration took place during a residency with the Greenville Symphony Orchestra on the part of Shaw and the Atlanta Symphony Orchestra, which was funded by the National Endowment for the Arts and South Carolina Arts Commission, in addition to funds from the Greenville Symphony Association and Furman University.[58] The concert that resulted from this collaboration included the "Prelude and Liebestod" from Richard Wagner's *Tristan und Isolde, Symphonic Metamorphoses on Themes by Carl Maria von Weber* by Paul Hindemith, "Nänie," by Johannes Brahms, and "Prologue to *Mefistofele*" by Arrigo Boito.[59] Shaw's appearance attracted a great deal of attention and Miriam Godspeed, writing in *The Greenville News*, wrote favorably of Furman Singers and their conductor.[60]

Figure 5.11 – Robert Shaw in rehearsal with Furman Singers and the Greenville Symphony Orchestra. Photo courtesy Furman Singers Archives.

Three governors of South Carolina have honored Furman Singers by selecting the ensemble to serve during their inaugural ceremonies. The first of these men was Richard Riley, Furman University class of 1954, who was elected to office in 1979. Furman Singers sang the hymn "God of Grace and God of Glory" with the Furman Brass Ensemble. Singers again performed for a governor entering his first term of office in 1999, this time singing alongside soprano Jessye Norman. The Furman Band joined Furman Singers for the performance at the inauguration of Jim Hodges. Singers also performed for the inauguration of Mark Sanford, Jr., Furman University class of 1983, after his election to the office of governor in 2003 and 2007.

Furman Singers performed for the American Choral Directors Association on several occasions between 1970 and 2010, at state, regional, and national conventions. The first performance of Furman Singers at a convention took place in the spring of 1974 at the Southern Division Convention in Charlotte, North Carolina. Furman Singers performed at a national convention in the spring of 1983, taking a program largely comprised of polychoral music to performance in Nashville, Tennessee. The program included Adriano Willaert's "In Convertondo Dominus," Giovanni Gabrieli's "O Magnum Mysterium," Hans Leo Hassler's "Psalm 66," Ralph Vaughan Williams' "Psalm 148," and Randall Thompson's "Have Ye Not Known?" and "Ye Shall Have a Song" from *The Peaceable Kingdom*. The performance was lauded by American Choral Directors Association leadership as exemplary of the best in repertoire and performance practice among college choirs. Maurice Casey, president-elect of the organization, was particularly effusive:

> I must...mention that your selection of literature was of the highest quality. You have had a significant impact on the

hundreds of persons who heard your performance. Thank you also for being prompt and punctual and polite. Please share with your singers and your superiors that most worthy was the respect and dignity shown by your singers to the other choirs and their members. This is witness to all that ACDA stands for.[61]

The performance attracted the attention of the South Carolina legislature as well, which passed a joint resolution of congratulations: "Congratulations to the Furman Singers of Furman University and their director, Dr. Bingham Vick, Jr., for being selected to perform for the national convention of the American Choral Directors Association in March, 1983, in Nashville, Tennessee."[62] Furman Singers next performed for the American Choral Directors Association national convention in San Antonio, Texas in 1987. In this performance Furman Singers joined the San Antonio Symphony and Northeast Missouri State University Singers in a concert conducted by Elmer Iseler. The program included Ralph Vaughan Williams' *Dona Nobis Pacem* and Srul I. Glick's *The Hour Has Come.* Writers for Furman University's student newspaper *The Paladin* contacted Colleen Kirk, who had taken part in the audition committee for that year's convention and commented, "It was really quite an honor to be selected to perform at the convention and it's especially noteworthy to appear twice in such a short time…Furman's choir obviously had everything we were looking for."[63] Furman Singers performed at conventions of the American Choral Director's Association on four more occasions during Vick's tenure: a clinic on Humor in Choral Music at the 1994 Southern Division convention in Knoxville, Tennessee, an interest session at the 1998 Southern Division convention in Charleston, South Carolina, at which Furman Singers also took part in an intercollegiate presentation of works by Leonard Bernstein under the baton of Dennis Schrock; the 2002 Southern Division convention in Charlotte, North Carolina; and the Southern Division convention in Memphis, Tennessee, in 2010 during the final spring semester of Vick's career at Furman University.

Among the more remarkable performances of Furman Singers during the same period was a series of collaborations with the Boston Pops and conductor Keith Lockhart. Lockhart is a Furman University alumnus of the class of 1981 and was the newly appointed conductor of the Boston Pops in the winter of 1995. At that time Lockhart visited Furman University's campus to work with the music department's various ensembles. In a conversation with Bingham Vick, Jr., Vick mentioned that Lockhart should keep Furman Singers in mind should he need a good chorus for collaboration. Vick's suggestion was somewhat playful, but Lockhart was facing the dilemma of finding a chorus for the summer of 1996 and the annual Boston Pops Fourth of July celebration and proposed that Furman Singers travel to Boston for the event that summer. Vick was intrigued and pleased with the suggestion and the two began planning in collaboration with Dennis Alves, Director of Artistic Programming for the Boston Pops, and Martha Vaughn of Furman University's administrative offices.

For Furman Singers and Furman University, Lockhart's invitation meant exposure to a huge live audience as well as national broadcast on the A&E Television Network. The stage on which the performance took place could only accommodate 75 singers, so, much as with the annual spring tour's limited bus space, Vick selected 75 singers from the larger ensemble. The members of the ensemble who were able to attend flew to Boston on July 1, 1996, to check into their hotel. Rehearsals followed on July 2 and July 3, with the performance on a rainy July 4 evening.

Figure 5.12 – Furman Singers, Bingham Vick, Jr., and Keith Lockhart. Photo courtesy Furman Singers Archives.

Though Dennis Alves expressed initial feelings of ambivalence regarding the collaboration, the resulting experience proved immensely satisfying for all parties. *The Boston Globe* and *The Boston Herald* covered the performance, as did *The Greenville News*. The two Boston papers complained of the secondary role of the Boston Pops at the evening's performance, but wrote positively of the visiting chorus. Richard Dyer, writing for *The Boston Globe*, focused the favorable portions of his review on Furman Singers, noting that the ensemble "produced a fervent, well tuned, and handsomely blended" performance for the audience of more than 200,000.[64]

Furman Singers collaborated on two more occasions with the Boston Pops, in 2006 and 2008. On both occasions the Furman Singers sang with the Boston Pops while the organization was engaged in its Christmas tour as well as a performance at Furman University's Timmons Arena. The events at Timmons Arena were substantial affairs, each involving a budget of more than $125,000 and months of planning. Though the timing of the concerts involved juggling the university's final examination schedule and a busy season for students in general, Vick took advantage of Dennis Alves' offer to have the Furman Singers accompany the Boston Pops on as many tour stops as seemed manageable. During the 2006 series of performances, Furman Singers appeared in several states with the Boston Pops to very favorable reviews. Composer Daniel Gawthrop, writing in his blog *Obblogato* for Dunstan House publishing company, noted the professionalism of Furman Singers in the rehearsal process: Furman Singers "went from sight-reading to final polish in a single two-hour rehearsal, which was a textbook example of how an efficient and purposeful rehearsal should be run."[65] Other newspaper columnists scattered across the tour's path praised Furman Singers and their director, as well.[66] Alves and Vick were pleased with the tour as well, and in the following summer set to work planning another such collaboration, initially considering Christmas of 2007 but settling on Christmas of 2008.

Furman Singers International Tours

Among the innovations Bingham Vick, Jr., instituted in the activity of Furman Singers was the ensemble's biennial trip abroad beginning in the summer of 1974. Since that time Furman Singers has taken a biennial trip to Europe or Asia without interruption. These tours extend from one to two weeks and involve performances in some of the most beautiful and historic venues of the countries in which they take place, extending Furman Singers' and Furman University's reputation internationally. The first opportunity for such a trip came with the auspices of the Romanian government and the U.S. Department of State.[67]

Furman Singers undertook a tour of Romania in that summer as part of the Ambassadors for Friendship program of cultural exchange. The program's founder, Harry Morgan, designed it to improve relations between the United States and Eastern Europe by providing incentive funds to American collegiate singing ensembles hoping to tour Romania. It began in 1971 with tours to Czechoslovakia. In 1974 Furman Singers was one of 25 ensembles selected for the honor. To prepare for the trip, Furman Singers engaged in a strenuous set of extra rehearsals during March, April, and May of the spring semester 1974. The ensemble also held rehearsals immediately prior to departure on July 31 and August 1 and 2. In addition to the funds provided by the program, the participants paid a substantial portion of the cost and raised additional monies through fundraising projects and a benefit concert on March 12, 1974.

The trip proved to be a difficult one, as the infrastructure and experience of the Romanian people were not in many ways suited to an American chorus, none of whom spoke Romanian. Vick recalls endless logistical difficulties, including being separated from some of his ensemble in different hotels in different locations with no phone service. Romanian audiences received Furman Singers warmly, however, and rushed forward with gratitude at the conclusion of each concert to receive the small United States flags Furman Singers provided to audiences as souvenirs. The tour happened to coincide with the resignation of United States President Richard Nixon. In the wake of the resignation Vick and members of Furman Singers faced questions from their Romanian audiences regarding what would happen next in the United States, apparently expecting that the country might devolve into a state of chaos as its leadership transitioned. The moment of defeat for Nixon became a moment for Furman Singers to share their account of the structure, organization, and stability of the United States government with Romanian audiences.

In 1976 Furman Singers toured Germany and Austria and followed that tour with a 1978 visit to Great Britain. On the latter trip Greenville WFBC-TV Channel 4's reporter Matt Hunt and cameraman Micky Hancock accompanied the ensemble, documenting the tour in the one-hour special "Their Finest Hour," which aired on Channel 4 twice, the following November and December, 1976. Vick and Furman Singers enjoyed the trip, and the documentary received praise from Furman University alumni and television producers alike.[68] The 1980 tour included travel to Germany, Austria, and Italy. Furman Singers toured England and France in 1982 with the benefit of letters of introduction from a wide range of political figures prominent in South Carolina and the United States, including United States Senators Strom Thurmond and Ernest F. Hollings, as well as Governor Richard W. Riley.[69]

In what would become one of their most storied tours of Europe and Asia, Furman Singers traveled to the Soviet Union and Estonia in 1990. The tour was significant in its timing, as Eastern Europe and the Soviet Union of the early 1990s constituted a rapidly changing political climate. Furman Singers was scheduled to sing at Gorky Park on the tour, but due to rainy conditions were forced to forego the concert in favor of additional time touring the Kremlin. One of the stops inside the Kremlin included the Dormition Cathedral, also known as the Cathedral of the Assumption, the mother church of the Russian Muscovites. While touring the cathedral, Vick asked if they might be allowed to perform a song so that his singers might experience the remarkable acoustics of the church. The tour guides agreed and, a bit later, also agreed to allow Furman Singers to perform the entirety of their sacred tour repertoire in light of the lack of improvement in the weather and cancellation of the Gorky Park concert. A tourism official from within the Kremlin interrupted the impromptu concert, but not before Furman Singers had performed much of its tour repertoire. According to the tour guide and the reporting of *The Greenville News*, the performance marked the first sacred music performed in the cathedral since the February Revolution of 1917.[70]

Figure 5.13 – Furman Singers in the Cathedral of the Assumption. Photo courtesy Furman Singers Archives.

Though the audiences in modern Russia and Estonia had varied reactions to renditions of Russian sacred music, they received performances of folks songs, spirituals, and patriotic music of the United States with a great deal of enthusiasm as reported by Colin Campbell of *The Atlanta Journal and Constitution*, who happened on the ensemble during a tour of Talinn.[71] Vick found this preference to be true of audiences in many countries: an affection for music by composers native to the country in which Furman Singers toured, but unbridled enthusiasm for performances of American folk songs, spirituals, and patriotic music. Over the course of 36 years of touring with Vick, the Furman Singers visited more than a dozen countries, including Great Britain, France, Spain, Estonia, Denmark, Finland, Poland,

Hungary, the Czech Republic, Germany, Austria, Switzerland, Italy, and Russia.

The Furman Singers Alumni Association
Among the most significant developments of the years from 1970 to 2010 was the emergence of an organized and motivated alumni network. Vick began the process of mobilizing the alumni of Furman Singers, whose numbers were approaching 2,000, with the 1979 reunion. This reunion involved DuPre Rhame's return to the podium to conduct after nine years of retirement as well as the performance of several favorites from the tenures of Rhame and Vick. The performance took the form of a worship service at The First Baptist Church of Greenville on June 10. Selections included W.A. Mozart's "Ave Verum Corpus," Franz Schubert's "The Omnipotence," Gustav Holst's "Psalm 148," and Roy Ringwald's arrangement of "The Battle Hymn of the Republic." Vick planned the event as a biennial affair, alternating with the Furman Singers tour overseas.

The 1979 reunion proved to be Rhame's final event conducting Furman Singers. He passed away in 1981, but his memory was the focus of a Furman University event in 1981 entitled "Horseplay" as well as the 1981 Furman Singers reunion. Furman Singers from classes spanning the years from 1947 through 1984 spent the reunion sharing stories, laughter, and tears. The reunion weekend again culminated in a worship service at First Baptist Church and included Thomas's Tallis' "If Ye Love Me," G.F. Handel's "Hallelujah Chorus," and Ralph Vaughan Williams' "O Clap Your Hands." In the intervening years the Furman Singers reunions most often took place at The First Baptist Church of Greenville, South Carolina, but also took place at Pendleton Street Baptist Church in Greenville on a few occasions and on two occasions during the Piccolo Spoleto Festival in Charleston, South Carolina, in 1993 and 2007. The 2009 reunion, taking place as it did in the summer before Vick's final year as director of Furman Singers, became a celebration of the conductor and his many accomplishments. More than 300 former Furman Singers attended the reunion, combining to form an enormous choir that filled the choir loft and much of the sanctuary of The First Baptist Church of Greenville, South Carolina.

Figure 5.14 – A button given at the 1995 Furman Singers reunion. Buttons expressing loyalty to DuPre Rhame read "DuPre Directed Me." Photo courtesy Furman Singers Archives.

As mentioned with regard to the fundraising for and construction of the Herring Music Pavilion, the Furman Singers alumni became, initially through the organizational efforts of Vick, a powerful force of advocacy for Furman Singers. In 2007, following the reunion in Charleston, South Carolina, Furman Singers alumni organized into the Furman Singers Alumni Association, the first of its kind on Furman University's campus, electing Sarah Bell, Furman University class of 1977 as its first president.[72] Goals of the association included further organization of and communication with Furman Singers alumni, assistance with the organization of the biennial reunions, and plans for a possible European trip for Furman Singers alumni. These duties had previously fallen to Vick.

Figure 5.15 – This portrait of Vick hangs in the lobby of the Herring Pavilion. Photo courtesy Furman Singers Archives.

Part of the organizational process for the group involved the unanimous adoption of extensive bylaws by the Furman Singers Alumni Association Board, ratified on June 8, 2007.[73] In addition to the purely organizational accomplishments of the group, in 2010 the board announced the completion of fundraising for the Judith S. and Bingham L. Vick, Jr. Professorship of Music, an effort that resulted in the establishment of a $1,250,000 endowed professorship in honor of Judy and Bingham Vick, Jr.[74] The resultant funds from the endowment will be used for the director of Furman Singers for salary enhancement, research support, professional development, and other purposes to be approved by the Provost and Executive Vice President of Furman University.

Bingham Vick, Jr.'s Retirement and Hugh Floyd

Much as with DuPre Rhame, Vick planned his retirement with care. In the final few years of his tenure he worked to make certain that he could conduct some of his favorite tour repertoire. He also saved his favorite major work for his final spring oratorio: J.S. Bach's *Mass in B Minor*. Perhaps most gratifying of all, Vick and Furman Singers performed for the 2010 Southern Division American Choral Directors Association Convention in Memphis, Tennessee to a theater filled with musicians, friends, and colleagues many of whom were aware of the nature of the performance: a 'goodbye' to this chapter in Vick's life. Vick presented a program quintessentially representative of the tour repertoire of Furman Singers over the years, blending some of the finest examples of art of the past, contemporary choral music, and folk song, spiritual, and gospel arrangements, including Orlando Gibbons' "O Clap Your Hands," Charles Stanford's "Beati Quorum Via," Z. Randall Stroupe's "Lamentations of Jeremiah" and Moses Hogan's "Music Down in My Soul," which served as the finale. During that last selection, Vick turned and interacted with the audience, who responded with great enthusiasm. He was visibly moved by the reception and the performance of Singers, who gave their all and performed beautifully. The atmosphere was one of celebration.

During that same spring semester, Vick, though he did not have a formal vote, sat alongside members of the Furman Singers Alumni Association, the Furman Music Department, and Furman administration on the selection process for his successor. Candidates included Furman Singers alumni, one of whom was Hugh Floyd, Furman University class of 1984. Floyd was, at that time, a tenured faculty member of the prestigious Oberlin College Conservatory of Music, where he taught from 1997 to 2010. After graduating from Furman, Floyd studied at the Eastman School of Music and University of Michigan. He also served as Director of Choral Activities and voice instructor for the Interlochen Center for the Arts and guest lecturer at Yale University. Floyd's college teaching experience and creative energy impressed the committee, and he accepted their offer for the position. In 2010, coinciding with his move to Furman, he was named Artistic Director for the New York State Summer School of the Arts School of Choral Studies.

Floyd faced a difficult task: until 2010 Furman Singers had only two conductors. Both conductors valued tradition and instilled the same sensibility in their students. Still, Floyd was well suited to the task of taking the helm of a program of long-standing traditions and excellence, having done so twice before. To begin, he invited Vick to rehearsals, accepted advice and input, and acknowledged Vick's contributions on many occasions. In Vick's words, "The spirit and enjoyment of the Singers experience continues quite strong. Hugh's repertoire is extensive, expansive, and inclusive. The Singers still have that wonderful sound and soul in their performances. Both

Judy and I could not be more pleased...It makes me feel good knowing Singers is in the hands of one who loves them." Floyd continued Singers spring tour, picnics in his back yard, carols at Christmas, a spring banquet, and continued support to Singers institutions such as the Mosquitoes and Honeybees, though he did not sing with them.

As a former Furman Singer, Floyd is poised to continue many of the established traditions of the ensemble. He inherits a legacy of excellence as well as tools wrought by years of hard work on the part of Rhame, Vick, and Furman Singers: secure sources of funds, impeccable rehearsal space, and a library of fine repertoire. He will also, just as with his two predecessors, mark Furman Singers with the imprint of his own personality. Undoubtedly Furman Singers has already left its mark on his life.

During the intervening years Singers has continued to perform at many functions on campus, continued to provide the chorus for fall and spring performances of masterworks including *Messiah*, and continued intermittent travel abroad. Singers toured Austria in 2012 and Germany in 2016. In the fall of 2016 a group of Singers traveled to New York City to perform with Kristen Chenoweth in her Broadway production *My Love Letter to Broadway*. Wherever it performs, the ensemble garners praise as one of the finest of its kind. As ambassadors for the university, as a focal point for proud and supportive alumni, and perhaps most importantly as a source of great beauty, Furman Singers continues in excellence.

---

1 Linney, interview; Parker, 35.
2 "Choral Ensembles at Furman." Furman Singers Archives, Greenville, South Carolina, 1969; "Choral Ensembles at Furman." Furman Singers Archives, Greenville, South Carolina, 1970; "Choral Ensembles at Furman." Furman Singers Archives, Greenville, South Carolina, 1971.
3 "The Northwestern University Music Department." Furman Singers Archives, Greenville, South Carolina, undated. The author found this copy of Margaret Hillis's

handbook alongside the Furman Singers handbook for the 1970 to 1971 school year. Bingham Vick, Jr., phone interview by author, May 9, 2011, Digital Recording.
4 "Furman University Singers: 1972-1973." Furman Singers Archives, Greenville, South Carolina, 1972.
5 "Furman University Singers: 1988-1989." Furman Singers Archives, Greenville, South Carolina, 1988.
6 "Furman University Singers: 2000-2001." Furman Singers Archives, Greenville, South Carolina, 2000.
7 "Constitution of the Furman University Singers." Furman Singers Archives, Greenville, South Carolina, 1978.
8 "The Furman University Singers: 1982-1983." Furman Singers Archives, Greenville, South Carolina, 1982.
9 Bingham Vick, Jr. "Singers," Furman Singers Archives, Greenville, South Carolina, undated. The author located these notes in a file marked "1974" and, in examining the context clues within the document, deduced the time frame in which it was written.
10 Bingham Vick, Jr., letter to Furman Singers officers, August 28, 1974; Bingham Vick, Jr. Student survey, Furman Singers Archives, Greenville, South Carolina, 1975.
11 Bingham Vick, Jr., letter to Alan Fulmer, July 8, 1975; Bingham Vick, Jr., letter to Mimi Schneider, July 14, 1975; Bingham Vick, Jr., Bingham Vick, Jr., letter to Keith Jones, July 14, 1975.
12 Vick, letter to Fulmer.
13 Vassy, interview; James E. Williams, III, phone interview by author, June 1, 2011, Digital Recording.
14 Williams, interview.
15 Williams, interview.
16 "Goals for Furman Singers: 1992-1993," Furman Singers Archives, Greenville, South Carolina, fall, 1992; "Furman Singers Officers' Meeting," Furman Singers Archives, Greenville, South Carolina, fall, 1995.
17 "Goals for Furman Singers: 1992-1993;" "The Furman University Singers: 2004-2005." Furman Singers Archives, Greenville, South Carolina, 2004.
18 Gordon W. Blackwell, Furman University's President, quoted in "Daniel Gives Furman $4 Million." *Furman Reports*, January, 1973.
19 Vick, letter to Fulmer.
20 Vassy, interview; Bingham Vick, Jr., email to the author, April 26, 2011; Gordon and Sarah Herring, interview.
21 L.A. Newkirk. "$1 Million Gift for Music Pavilion to Boost Furman." *The Greenville News,* September 19, 1995.
22 *Messiah*. Concert Program. Furman Singers Archives, Greenville, South Carolina, 1970.
23 Thomas Mosely. "*Messiah* Returns to Handel's Tradition at FU Sunday." *The Greenville News*, December 4, 1970.
24 Vick, quoted in Parker, 39.
25 John Crabtree, letter to Bingham Vick, Jr., July 8, 1981.
26 Bingham Vick, Jr., letter to Furman Singers, May 18, 1982.
27 Sharon Todd. "Bach is Back – P.D.Q., That Is." *The Greenville News*, May 15, 1977.

28 *The Music of P.D.Q. Bach.* Concert Program. Furman Singers Archives, Greenville, South Carolina, 1977.
29 Bingham Vick, Jr., letter to Peter Schickele, February 17, 1993; Peter Schickele, letter to Bingham Vick, Jr., March 10, 1993; Peter Schickele, letter to Bingham Vick, Jr., December 8, 1993.
30 Peter Schickele, letter to Bingham Vick, Jr., April 16, 1993.
31 Staci Sturrock. "P.D.Q.: A Chip Off the Old Bach." *The Greenville News,* April 23, 1995.
32 "Lecture Demonstration: Humor in Choral Music," Furman Singers Archives, Greenville, South Carolina, February 6, 1999.
33 William Thomas, email to Bingham Vick, Jr., April 21, 1995; Vick, interview, June 6, 2011.
34 Bingham Vick, Jr., letter to Edwin Irey, January 29, 1971.
35 Bingham Vick, Jr., letter to Paul Langston, October 11, 1971; Paul Langston, letter to Bingham Vick, Jr., October 15, 1971; Bingham Vick, Jr., letter to W. Michael Chertok, January 15, 1971.
36 Bingham Vick, Jr., letter to Lloyd Landrum, December 14, 1970.
37 Edwin S. Irey, letter to Bingham Vick, Jr., January 15, 1970.
38 Bingham Vick, Jr., letter to Edward S. French, January 12, 1971; Bingham Vick, Jr., letter to Edwin Irey, November 5, 1970.
39 Paul Langston, letter to Bingham Vick, Jr., March 12, 1971.
40 Lloyd Landrum, letter to Bingham Vick, Jr., March 8, 1971.
41 Edward S. French, letter to Bingham Vick, Jr., March 22, 1971.
42 DuPre Rhame, telegram to Bingham Vick, Jr. and Furman Singers, 1971.
43 Troupe Harris, letter to Bingham Vick, Jr., January 21, 1972.
44 R.D. Roberts, letter to Bingham Vick, Jr., January 6, 1972.
45 Schoonmaker, interview.
46 "Key to the City," Furman Singers Archives, Greenville, South Carolina, 1974.
47 Vick, letter to Fullmer; Vick, letter to Schneider.
48 Marilyn Schneider, letter to President Gerald Ford, August 14, 1975; Marilyn Schneider, letters to Congressman James R. Mann, Senator Strom Thurmond, and Senator Ernest F. Hollings, August 15, 1975; Bingham Vick, Jr., letter to President Gerald Ford, August 14, 1975; Bingham Vick, Jr., letters to Congressman James R. Mann, Romanian Ambassador to the United States, Corneliu Bogdan, Senator Strom Thurmond, and Ernest F. Hollings, February 19, 1975.
49 Joe Short, letter to Bingham Vick, Jr., March 12, 1975.
50 W. Richard Wynn, letter to Bingham Vick, Jr., March 7, 1984.
51 Bingham Vick, Jr., letter to Jacques M. Kearns, October 6, 1983.
52 "Bus Costs," Furman Singers Archives, Greenville South Carolina, 1989. A note, written in Vick's hand, detailing bus costs for tour between 1970 and 1989 and projecting costs for 1990. "Tour Expenses," Furman Singers Archives, Greenville, South Carolina, 1989. A summary of tour expenses prepared for John Crabtree and Charlotte Smith. Bingham Vick, Jr., letter to John Crabtree, September 11, 1989; John Crabtree, letter to Bingham Vick, Jr., 11 September 11, 1989.
53 Bingham Vick, Jr., letter to John Crabtree, March 12, 1990; Bingham Vick, Jr., letter to John Johns, April 1, 1991.

54 Bingham Vick, Jr., letter to John Crabtree and Charlotte Smith, September 26, 1989.
55 Charlotte Smith, letter to Bingham Vick, Jr., 1980.
56 Charlotte Smith, letter to Bingham Vick, Jr., March 10, 1988.
57 Bingham Vick, Jr., letter to Furman Singers, May 23, 1990; also, Bingham Vick, Jr., letter to Skyland Singers, Kathy Cochran, director, May 21, 1990; Bingham Vick, Jr., letter to Robert Tyson, May 21, 1990.
58 Bingham Vick, Jr., letter to Furman University music faculty, January 3, 1973; "Daniel Gives Furman $4 Million." *Furman Reports,* January, 1973.
59 *The Greenville Symphony Orchestra.* Concert Program. Furman Singers Archives, Greenville, South Carolina, 1973.
60 "What's Doing: Joint Concert Equals Last Year's Event." *The Greenville News,* January 12, 1973.
61 Maurice Casey, letter to Bingham Vick, Jr., March 21, 1983.
62 "Concurrent Resolution by State Senators Theodore, Chapman, Richardson, Verne, Smith, and Taylor." Furman Singers Archives, Greenville, South Carolina, January 11, 1983.
63 "Furman Singers Perform." *The Paladin,* March 20, 1987.
64 Richard Dyer. "Up-tempo Night for a TV Crowd." *The Boston Globe,* July 5, 1996.
65 Daniel Gawthrop. Obblogato, entry posted November 29, 2006, http://www.dunstanhouse.com/blog/ [accessed June 5, 2011].
66 Edward Clark. "Pops Concert Brings Peaceful Feeling." *The Advocate-Messenger,* December 7, 2006; Geraldine Freeman. "Pops Bring Holiday Cheer to Proctor's Performance." *The Daily Gazette,* November 30, 2006; Tricia Olszewski. "Boston Pops." *The Washington Post,* December 2, 2006.
67 Bingham Vick, Jr., letter to Furman University administration, November 2, 1973.
68 "Furman Singers Tour Subject for Documentary." *The Baptist Courier,* July 6, 1978; Dave Partridge, letter to Bingham Vick, Jr., September 6, 1978; Basil Manly IV, letter to Bingham Vick, Jr., September 12, 1978; Charles T. Gaines, letter to Bingham Vick, Jr., September 4, 1978; W. Marvin Gravely, letter to Bingham Vick, Jr., September 6, 1978.
69 Ernest F. Hollings, letter of introduction for Furman Singers, July 29, 1981; Strom Thurmond, letter of introduction for Furman Singers, August 17, 1981; Richard W. Riley, letter of introduction for Furman Singers, August 12, 1981.
70 131 Vick, interview, May 9, 2011; "Furman Singers Perform in Kremlin Cathedral." *The Poinsett Register,* September 8, 1990.
71 Colin Campbell. "Hallelujah in the Baltics." *The Atlanta Journal and Constitution,* August 19, 1990.
72 Sarah Bell. "A Note from the President." *Encore: Furman Singers Alumni Newsletter,* Fall, 2007.
73 "Furman Singers Alumni Association Bylaws." Furman Singers Archives, Greenville, South Carolina, 2007.
74 "Statement of Understanding for the Judith S. and Bingham L. Vick, Jr. Professorship of Music." Furman Singers Archives, Greenville, South Carolina, 2010

CHAPTER 6

ALWAYS MAKE MUSIC: AN EXAMINATION OF THE TOUR REPERTOIRE OF FURMAN SINGERS

Choral activity at Furman University has included concert tours as part of its focus since the early years of the school's glee club tradition, as outlined in Chapter 3. Touring served several purposes, including the improvement of Furman University's local, regional, and national profile, the promotion of its music program, entertaining and edifying audiences, showcasing the school's musical activity to prospective students and alumni, and providing focus and a creative outlet for current students. The repertoire for the tours of Furman Singers reveals much regarding its conductors' philosophies of curriculum planning and aesthetic goals. The ensuing discussion examines the various genres of the tour repertoire of Furman University Singers, the time periods represented by repertoire selections, the frequency of performance in terms of genre and time period, and consideration of the possible influences on repertoire selection.

DuPre Rhame and the Music of the Stage

DuPre Rhame's repertoire selections centered on music drawn from opera and operetta. The 1948 season, the first year in which Rhame and Furman Singers undertook a regional tour, provides an excellent example. Rhame programmed selections from Benjamin Godard's *Jocelyn,* Giuseppe Verdi's *Rigoletto,* Modeste Mussorgsky's *Boris Godunov,* and Gilbert and Sullivan's *The Gondoliers.* Together, these selections represented nearly one-third of the tour concert. Rhame dedicated the remainder of the program to standards of contemporary church repertoire and arrangements of glee club favorites. An arrangement of Schubert's "Ave Maria," two choruses from G.F. Handel's *Messiah,* and Nicola Antonio's "Go Not Far from Me, O God" numbered among the sacred selections. The glee club standards included "Brothers, Sing On" by Edward Grieg and "The Whiffenpoof Song" by Rudy Vallee. Remarkably, proportions of the 1948 spring concert remained consistent for much of Rhame's career as director of Furman Singers.

As a percentage of the total of Furman Singers repertoire between 1948 and 1970, repertoire taken from opera, operetta, or musicals accounted for approximately one-third of that material. Western art music of the Renaissance, Baroque, Classical, and Romantic eras was featured only slightly less often. Sacred choral compositions, both original and arrangements of hymns, made up approximately one-sixth of Furman Singers repertoire. Glee club arrangements such as the aforementioned "Whiffenpoof Song" of Rudy Vallee made up around one-tenth of Furman Singers repertoire, and spiritual arrangements comprised only a very minor component. In fact, though spiritual arrangements had been a staple of glee clubs and choruses for decades by the time of the founding of Furman Singers, as exhibited by the repertoire of Furman University's own glee clubs from 1902 through 1930, spirituals appeared on only seven of the concerts surveyed.

The repertoire of Rhame's second tour marked another of his affinities: repetition. Rhame did not shy from programming the same work in proximate school years. Harry Simeone's choral transcription of Tchaikovsky's *Nutcracker Suite*, for example, featured on tours in 1949, 1950, and 1954. Rhame programmed Livingston Gearhart's arrangement of "Dry Bones," which had been highlighted in Furman University's student newspaper as of particular interest to the student body, in 1948, 1949, and 1950. Johannes Brahms's "How Lovely Is Thy Dwelling Place" from his *German Requiem* found a place on tours in 1950 and 1952. Rhame programmed Jane M. Marshall's "My Eternal King" in 1962, 1964, and 1967. Other examples of repertoire repeated within a short span abound. Rhame also utilized tour as an opportunity to showcase selections from the spring opera of the previous year or the coming spring performance.

In addition to the likelihood that audiences would know and remember these favored selections, presumably the repetition of repertoire allowed Rhame extra rehearsal time, both for the preparation of other selections for tour and for the spring opera, which followed very closely after tour. Some repetition represented the establishment of Furman Singers traditions, however, as was the case with both Rhame's arrangement of "Brown Eyes" and, under Vick's tenure, the performance of Roy Ringwald's arrangement of "The Battle Hymn of the Republic." Ringwald's setting featured on tour in 1948 and became a favorite of Furman Singers and the ensemble's audiences early in Rhame's tenure. Bingham Vick, Jr., sensitive to the power of such continuity and tradition, programmed "The Battle Hymn of the Republic" for every tour from 1970 through 2010.

Rhame's repertoire selections likely reflected his personal experience as a singer. Having studied vocal performance and worked as a performer, Rhame would have known the music of opera, operetta, and the American musical very well. Rhame also needed to consider the particular audiences who would be interested in the activity of Furman Singers. For the most part, these were congregations of Southern Baptists in the southeast. Sacred choral music represented a minority of Rhame's selections, but it is notable that Rhame's programming, in the case of art music, favored those pieces that were both sacred and accessible for congregations and the choirs assembled from those congregations, such as J.S. Bach's "Jesu, Joy of Man's Desiring," Ludwig Van Beethoven's "Hallelujah," W.A. Mozart's "Ave Verum Corpus," and Michael Praetorius' "Lo, How a Rose E'er Blooming."

Bingham Vick, Jr. and the Western Art Music Tradition

Bingham Vick, Jr., like DuPre Rhame, programmed selections reflecting his background. While at Northwestern University, Vick studied for and earned a master's degree in vocal performance; but, after completing that degree, Vick studied for a Ph.D. in music history and choral literature. It should hardly be surprising that fully half of the repertoire Vick programmed for Furman Singers between 1970 and 2010 is part of the western art music tradition. Almost one-fifth of that repertoire, however, is music written by composers contemporaneous with Furman Singers, including artists such as Arvo Pärt, Morten Lauridsen, Daniel Gawthrop, David Schwoebel, and Z. Randall Stroupe. Composers from the Romantic era and earlier make up about one-third of Vick's selections.

One of the challenges facing Vick as a young conductor was finding the right balance of art music and lighter fare, what Vick would eventually term the "Lighter Side" of Furman Singers. Vick's first tour season favored art music, with selections by well-known composers of the Renaissance, Baroque, Classical, Romantic, and Modern eras accounting for all but three pieces on the concert. In 1972 Vick moderated this tendency; only half of the tour concert was art music. The other half of the concert material was either arrangements of folk songs and spirituals or part of a set of arrangements of Burt Bacharach favorites, including "What the World Needs Now Is Love" and "Close to You." The 1973 concert was again split into halves along these lines. In 1974 composers such as J.S. Bach, Jan Pieterszoon Sweelinck, W.A. Mozart, G.F. Handel, Anton Bruckner, Hugo Wolf, and Francis Poulenc comprised slightly more than half of the repertoire. Eventually the ratio settled into the balance mentioned above: somewhat more than two-thirds of each concert was devoted to art music and choral settings of hymn tunes, spirituals, and folk songs. The final third of each concert featured popular music, jazz, and performances by the Mosquitoes and Honeybees. Over the course of Vick's entire career with Furman Singers arrangements of popular music, humorous music, and jazz accounted for around one-fifth of the repertoire. Settings of hymns and folk songs together made up approximately one tenth of the repertoire. Spiritual arrangements, popular with audiences and singers alike, made up another tenth.

Like DuPre Rhame, and like many conductors of the a cappella choir tradition, Vick repeated repertoire with some regularity, especially repertoire that had proven popular or delivered particularly successful performances. Over 40 years of programming, Furman Singers performed some pieces several times. Vick seems to have been most open to repeated performances of selections from the standard art music repertoire. Other than "Brown Eyes" and Roy Ringwald's "Battle Hymn of the Republic," Johannes Brahms' motet "Schaffe in mir, Gott, ein rein Herz" was one of Furman Singers' two most frequently performed selections. It was featured on seven different concerts in 1977, 1980, 1984, 1988, 1992, 2001, and 2006. Vick repeated performances of favorite arrangements as well: Furman Singers performed James Erb's "Shenandoah" on concerts in 1984, 1985, 1988, 1991, 1995, 2001, and 2006. Alberto

Ginastera's "Lamentaciones de Jeremias Propheta" appeared on concerts in 1971, 1977, 1982, 1991, 1995, and 2007. Vick was less willing than Rhame to repeat repertoire from one year to the next, however, and seldom programmed the same piece in two subsequent seasons. In most cases Vick tended to guarantee that no single student would perform a selection more than once in a typical four-year undergraduate experience. Over the course of his 40 years as director of the ensemble, Vick, on average, programmed ten new selections per year, for a total of nearly 400 unique selections.

Vick often faced questions from church leaders regarding his programming, especially in the case of music in languages other than English. In 1983, in a letter answering such concerns raised by Jacques M. Kearns, minister of music at The First Baptist Church of Augusta, Georgia, Vick articulated his programming philosophy:

> My approach to the Furman Singers tour repertoire has always been one of balance – hopefully, a "something for everyone" program – and inclusion of only the strongest examples of the finest church music from all historical periods. As a college choir, we seldom do much of the "standard church anthem" literature because that repertoire is presented regularly by the fine church choirs where we tour. I strive for the highest level of performance quality in such a spirit that the music of Brahms and Bach and Mozart – even when sung in German or Latin – communicates with all the audience, regardless of the various backgrounds and musical tastes.[1]

Vick also published his thoughts in his 2003 book on conducting: *Conducting: What Matters Most*. In the book, Vick devotes an entire chapter to repertoire and repertoire selection. The first thing he writes is that the "single most important task for a choral conductor is selecting repertoire for the choir."[2] He compares the concert program to a meal and urges the young conductor to choose repertoire representing a balanced diet of music from various historical periods and styles, new music, and music that is immediately satisfying or enjoyable. Vick also cites resources for repertoire selection, including the American Choral Directors Association website, the *Choral Journal,* several articles related to the African American spiritual, and articles about Russian sacred music.

---

1 Bingham Vick, Jr., letter to Jacques M. Kearns, October 6, 1983.
2 Bingham Vick, Jr. Conducting: What Matters Most, 121.

APPENDIX A

INTERVIEW TRANSCRIPTIONS

Interview, Bingham Vick, Jr., April 18, 2011

ROBERTSON: When you first came to Furman, you had a vision that included variety and inclusion of contemporary works as well as historically informed performance – I'm thinking of your first *Messiah* performance. Could you talk about those early days and what your vision was, where that vision was formed, and how it was influenced and worked out in those first few years?

VICK: One of the things that attracted me to Furman in the first place is that it was a Baptist institution. I was raised a Southern Baptist. My undergraduate experience was at Stetson University, which at that time...Stetson was to Florida what Furman was to South Carolina in terms of being the Baptist College. My experience at Stetson was very similar to what DuPre [Rhame] was doing at Furman. DuPre's counterpart at Stetson was Professor Harold Giffin, a very likable older gentleman. He had been at Stetson forever. He had a touring choir, did a lot of the same kind of literature that DuPre did with Furman Singers at Furman. So my undergraduate experience at Stetson was very similar to what DuPre was doing and what an undergraduate at Furman would be experiencing. So when I applied for the job, my conversations with DuPre were very congenial from the beginning, because I brought to the table a collegiate experience that was pretty much exactly what he was doing at Furman already, and I'm sure, for him, having founded Furman Singers, he was very concerned that whoever took over when he retired would not mess up what he had nurtured. So I think he felt good about me coming in because of that experience and I felt good about coming in because I was accustomed to that kind of touring choir undergraduate, collegiate atmosphere.

Coming fresh out of graduate school, I was very full of myself, and I had a very high-quality experience in choral music at Northwestern. I sang in the Chicago Symphony Chorus for several years. I was assistant conductor of the Symphony Chorus my last year there under Margaret Hillis. Northwestern was a very highly respected graduate school in terms of choral work. So I had a very high-powered, high-level professional graduate experience in choral music there, and I brought a lot of that experience to the table when I came to Furman.

I had just recently, at Northwestern, been a part of the performance of [Handel's] *Messiah*, for instance, that took the performance practice back to what Handel had experienced. Until the 50s and '60s the basic *Messiah* performance philosophy was bigger is better. *Messiah* had gone through several different orchestrations over the last 200 years, basically beefing up the orchestra, getting away from the Baroque orchestra and into a more Romantic, emotional, colorful orchestration. Robert Shaw came out with a new recording, going back to Baroque tempos, using just a Baroque orchestra of strings, oboes, bassoons, trumpets, and tympani in particular places, just as Handel had done. So I had just had that experience.

At Furman the tradition was to do *Messiah* every Christmas. DuPre combined his choir at First Baptist with Furman Singers and invited any Furman Singers alumni who wanted to just show up and sing. It was always done the same way. DuPre preferred the big,

Romantic orchestra; he brought in professional soloists from New York because he felt that only experienced, professional, adult singers could perform the *Messiah* performers with the intensity and the understanding and the expertise. Sidebar, I decided to use student soloists and that's one of the very few disagreements DuPre and I had. He let me know that he did not think students could do the job appropriately, and I responded that we're an educational institution and this is where students need to get this experience. He responded, I disagree with you, but I will support you because it's now your program. You're in charge. A mild disagreement, a philosophical disagreement.

So when I came in to Furman my first responsibility was *Messiah* at Christmas, and I immediately changed a number of things. We still used a large chorus; we did not invite Furman Singers alumni to just show up and sing; I pared the orchestra down to just strings, oboes, and bassoons, trumpets, and timpani where Handel wrote. My desire was to perform this *Messiah,* my first *Messiah* as a conductor, my first *Messiah* at Furman, to bring it back to the Baroque performing practice that most professional groups were moving toward.

I think *Messiah* can successfully be performed either way. It depends on what the intent of the performance is; it depends on what the intent of the conductor is. *Messiah* is a wonderful work and I've done it numerous times over the years with a variety of orchestrations. Its greatness lies in the fact that it cannot be destroyed [laughs] regardless of how strange you make it in terms of orchestration; but we did *Messiah*, in my estimation, a little closer to the way Handel would have expected it to be done. We used student soloists. It was a very successful first performance.

In general, when I came to Furman, I had spent some time studying the repertoire of Furman Singers. DuPre…in his era, the norm was to do basically what he did. In terms of tour repertoire, there would be some sort of great, old sacred anthems, chestnuts they were called. There would be some operatic duets and solos, there would be a piano solo in the program, there would be some spirituals, at some point there would be something of a lighter, entertaining nature. That was the norm. Coming out of my undergraduate experience and with my graduate experience and my young repertoire philosophy, I wanted to do, basically, a variety of great choral works: Renaissance, Baroque, Romantic, contemporary. Because our tours performed almost exclusively at churches, I felt the need to do all-sacred programs. In more recent years I've moved a little bit away from that, but in those early days I wanted to follow in the same traditional touring philosophy that DuPre had used in terms of where we sang and length of program, variety of program; but I wanted it all to be choral music and not operatic duets and other things.

So we jumped in and as with all young conductors, you do with your first choir what you have done in the past. Whatever you did previously you decide that now's the time for it to be done correctly and you're going to conduct it that way. So that was my philosophy. So in the early years I did a lot of things that I had done in high school, that I had done in college, that I had done in graduate work. This was pretty solid, basic choral repertoire in those years. High school choirs were expected to know Mendelssohn's "He Watching Over Israel," they were expected to have sung Randall Thompson's "Alleluia," they were expected to know Beethoven's "Hallelujah" from *Christ on the Mount of Olives*. That was standard repertoire, and that's what I brought to the table.

I do remember, the very first thing I conducted with Furman Singers was the "Hallelujah" from *Christ on the Mount of Olives*, because I was told we had to sing for convocation, which happened the first week of school, which gave me, I think, one rehearsal beforehand. Nancy Lyons was my accompanist; she was a senior that year, and she and I have been good and close friends and colleagues ever since. She was my accompanist, she was a piano major, she was handy at the organ. When I told her at one of the early officer meetings before school started that we would do the Beethoven "Hallelujah" she said, are you crazy? And I said, well probably, but that's what we're going to do.

The Singers were not accustomed to quite the level of rehearsal intensity that I expected. I think their general rehearsal philosophy was to have a good time and do good things, but, if it took a while to learn it, then it took a while to learn it. My approach was a little more we have this to do, we have this many minutes in which to learn it, we are going to work hard immediately to make that happen. So we did the Beethoven "Hallelujah" and the Singers sounded wonderful. I think, for the upper classmen in Singers, it was sort of a wakeup call to things being a little different in Singers.

Whenever an organization changes conductors, there's always going to be a difference; it's not necessarily better or worse. It can be better or worse, but it's going to be different. I think they realized that Singers were going to be musically different. I think in the early months the jury was still out as to whether it was going to be better or worse than things were before me, but I think in time they saw that when you work hard in rehearsals and you take care of details, the bigger picture comes into focus more clearly and more successfully.

I think I brought a slightly different repertoire philosophy, a slightly different rehearsal attitude and philosophy. I'm sure part of that was my youthful intensity. I found in my own career that the older I got, I became a little more mellow. I'm sure DuPre was that way. DuPre was 70 when he retired and I was 26. So for an ensemble to go from having a conductor at age 70 who had been there forever to a young whippersnapper age 26 was quite an adjustment for them on a number of levels. What I wanted them to understand from day one was that, while I was young, I had all the right answers [laughs], no, not really. But I wanted them to know that I knew what I was doing, that I was confident in what I wanted them to do and in the road that we needed to take to get where we were going. I invited them to get on board, and they did. The early years were lots of fun, very successful; we had a good time in rehearsals. I don't think anyone was so offended in the change that they did anything drastic. I'm sure there were some who did not to work as hard as I wanted them to work, but they did, and things went well.

ROBERTSON: Talk for just a bit about the transition between your tenure and DuPre Rhame's tenure.

VICK: Singers was his baby; he had created it; he had nurtured his own philosophy in it in terms of musical excellence, which he demanded. The organizational structure was his, and I'm sure this was…because this was the way it was at Stetson when I was there. We're a fine choir, but we're a family. This is a fraternity; this is a group of friends as well as a group of musicians as well as…There are some people there because they are required to be in an ensemble; there are some people there because they love to sing; there are some people there with great voices; there are some there with not-so-great voices, but they really want to be there. You know, it's a strange sort of mix, and DuPre fostered that family *esprit de corps* just as I had experience at Stetson, so I'm sure he felt very good knowing that, at least from our conversation, I wasn't trying to reassure him exactly, but I wanted to let him know that I understood a little bit about what he had done, and that was the way I planned to continue. I'm sure that made him feel good.

ROBERTSON: How much of a role did he play in terms of advising you or visibility in the community once he had retired?

VICK: He was wonderful. He let me know from the beginning that, if I had any questions or needed his advice, he was there, but he never approached me. Each fall I would invite him to rehearsal because I wanted the Singers to understand the continuity and the perspective of where Singers had come from. Every fall he would come at an appointed rehearsal and sit in. DuPre was a big, sort of Elijah kind of person. Deep, bass-baritone voice, big guy, relatively long white hair. You felt you were in the presence of a prophet or something, and at the end of rehearsal he would say a few words and inspire Singers to understand that there were three priorities in life. I can remember him saying this, and in this order: God, family, and Furman Singers. All else didn't matter. That should be their priority. And he believed that, and I do too! It hadn't worked quite that well with more things to occupy students' minds over the years, but that kind of allegiance and dedication and commitment and atmosphere was what he wanted to create. The students did that, they bought in to that, and I think that can be seen in the allegiance of the alumni to the reunions. There are people from the early 50s and 60s who come religiously to the Singers reunions because they still feel, now 65 years later, that same commitment, that same love, and that same love of being in Furman Singers. I think what he did was just tremendous, and I loved having him there to say to the students "this is how things are, young people. This is the greatest thing you're going to do in your whole life next to getting married, maybe. And perhaps getting married might not be all that great [laughs]." No, he didn't say that.

ROBERTSON: You've written that your philosophy of life and teaching is formed over the years and through experience. It sounds as if it drew heavily on your experience as an undergraduate. How did your philosophy of teaching and conducting change over the years?

VICK: I think teaching philosophy and musical philosophy in hindsight is hard to analyze. It seems to me that the successful conductors, the successful teachers…I guess you could apply this to anything. Business people, successful housewives. They start with some basic, bedrock premises or understanding and then you go from there.

For me the basic philosophy with Furman Singers, also with my church choir for 28 years, also with Greenville Chorale continuing now, is be true to the music. Do everything possible to understand the composer, the poetry, the intent of the composition, to understand, historically, the "what" and "why" and "where" and "how" the composer created something.

Secondly, to understand as thoroughly as possible the personnel, the talent you have to work with, their attitudes, their aspirations, their reasons for being there.

Thirdly, trying to bring together the best efforts of those people to perform, as closely as possible, the composer's intentions.

I think each of those steps can be expanded considerably. I think, for any ensemble, *esprit de corps* cannot be overestimated, whether you play football for the Atlanta Falcons or whether you sing in Furman Singers or whether you play basketball for the North Carolina Tarheels or whether you play in the Chicago Symphony

Orchestra. Certainly the individual talent is very important. The level of performing ability, the level of musicianship, all of those are very important if you're going to have a high-quality product; but then it's a team effort. Everybody's got to work together, and the more you can work together the better you are going to be able to perform. The more you enjoy being with the people who are sitting beside you in that rehearsal, the better you are going to perform. The better you know one another, the better you are going to perform. That may be just basic human nature, but I think when you know the person beside you is working very hard, you're willing to work very hard. When you know somebody's got your back, you're willing to get somebody else's back.

Doing things to foster a strong *esprit de corps* is just in the best interest of the performance down the road. It also makes for an enjoyable journey. I've had very little turnover in the Greenville Chorale. I've been conducting them now for 30 years. I think people stay and they put up with two hours of hard work on Monday night because I do my best to make it an enjoyable hurt [chuckles], to try to make it an enjoyable experience even though we are working hard, even though I may yell and scream at them from time to time, even though I push them as hard as possible. I know some are better voices than others. I think there's something incredibly positive when you are part of a winning team and, for a lot of people, for most people, they can't sing by themselves nearly well enough to stand on the stage of Carnegie Hall or some similar venue and have people applaud them. But when they're in a fine choir, even their less-than-outstanding talent can be recognized as a part of the larger whole. That's a real blessing, I think, for musicians.

If you have a choir of all exceptionally trained soloists with lots of degrees and lots of experience, they can sound phenomenal, as Robert Shaw proved. Or they can sound horrendous. If everybody's out for himself in a choral situation, it's not going to be a happy conclusion, but if they all are willing to be a part of the corporate effort, then it is successful. It's phenomenally successful. A lot of that has to do with *esprit de corps*.

I had that same sort of experience as an undergraduate and that's what I wanted to do with Furman Singers. I wanted us to be the best choir in the country, period, bar none. I wanted us to do great literature, I wanted us to do it musicologically correctly. I wanted us to do it beautifully, and I wanted to have a good time along the way. I think, for the most part, that's worked.

ROBERTSON: Could you talk about specifics, from your perspective that you did to foster that sense of *esprit de corps*?

VICK: Some of the thing I did I simply continued from what DuPre had done. The banquet at the end of the year being, maybe, the most obvious. It was always a dress-up affair. The girls wore long, formal dresses; the guys wore suits. It was a really high-class thing. In the early years we continued to go downtown to the Poinsett Hotel ballroom, which no longer is in existence. It was a big deal to honor the seniors. That's a good way to sort of wrap the year up and also to share feelings, and that's continued.

I wanted to do some things during the year that put us together outside of rehearsal, so at the beginning of the year we would have a picnic in our backyard. In the early years, the managers and I would actually fry hamburgers. The dining hall would supply food free because everybody was on a meal ticket and if they weren't eating at the dining hall, they would be eating with us. We got the whole enchilada and we had multiple grills and we would cook hamburgers for 130 people, and play some games and get to know one another. The freshmen were always the new kids on the block, and I wanted to do as much as possible as quickly as possible to get these new people into the family. I wanted them to feel like they were important, that they were a part of what we were doing, so whatever we could do to introduce them to each other and to the upperclassmen we wanted to do. In the fall we would always go to at least one or two football games together, just sit together at the ball game. It's got nothing to do with music. It had everything to do with let's get together just because we like being together and do stupid things at the football game, so we would.

At Christmas time, and I think DuPre did this, we would go Christmas caroling. That's a very obvious thing for a choir to do. We would go and sing for DuPre, we would go to a nursing home, there were always some special Furman people we would try to get to, and then wind up somewhere for a party, whether it was at our house or at a church basement or whatever. Again, an opportunity to get out of rehearsal, for people to do something as Furman Singers, as a unit, that was not necessarily music performance-oriented.

Over the years, once we lived so close and we had a nice basement with a fireplace, we would have little disco parties in our basement, dance parties. Get a fire going, have somebody bring over a boom-box, just a pure social occasion. Bring a date if you want to. We would put chairs around the wall, and you could sit and talk and munch on refreshments or dance or what have you. Just an opportunity to be together outside of rehearsal.

In the spring we started what turned into an annual Furman Singers versus the Band softball game. Singers always had to stay and sing for graduation. The Band was always there, so we started what became an annual tradition of playing the Band. It was girls and boys mixed teams, it was slow pitch, it was a lot of fun, it was crazy, free substitution. I think the first year Jay Bocook was in charge of the Furman Band. He and I thought that would be a good thing both for the Band and for Singers, and so we set it up and the Singers arrived to play. The girls in Singers who were going to play arrived in their cute little matching outfits with their hair beautifully coiffed, and the Band girls arrived wearing baseball cleats with their own gloves and black under their eyes. They killed us [laughs]. From then on, part of the audition process for Singers was something having to do with, do you play softball? But over the years we have defeated the Band on a fairly regular basis.

Another thing that we started, and I don't remember what year, since Singers had to sing for graduation and since exams were over before that, we started going to the beach as a group. When you would finish your last exam, you would truck down to Myrtle Beach and we would get a motel and we had maybe as many as 20 rooms. Absolutely no plan, absolutely no musical anything, just be at the beach for a few days, after exams were over, a chance to relax and sort of let your hair down. Then we would all troop back to Furman and sing for graduation, which was on Friday or Saturday or something. We had some great times. We did nothing as a group other than that we would gather sometime late in the afternoon and decide where we wanted to go eat. Then we would go mob some seafood place, or two or three seafood places. Play in the pool, beach football, whatever. It was just a time to be together, to enjoy each other's company, to just have fun, with no musical motive, no subtext, come when you can, stay as long as you can, everybody paid their own way. Back then you could get a room for 40 bucks or something so, for four people, that's 10 bucks a night. Judy and I would go get coffee and doughnuts and milk and breakfast was in our room. Just come down to our room and have a doughnut and a cup of coffee and a glass of milk and, again, it was just an opportunity to enjoy being together.

I think all of those things, from the banquet at the beginning of the year, the opening picnic, they all strengthened *esprit de corps* and fostered the family feel to being in Furman Singers.

ROBERTSON: Could you talk about the scholarships associated with Furman Singers?

VICK: When DuPre retired, the Furman Singers, with the help of some alumni, started the DuPre Rhame Scholarship. At that time it had to have $10,000 in the endowment before it was activated. It had about $5,000 when I arrived because DuPre had just retired. Over the next few years I did what I could to encourage additional gifts to that. I think the final gift came, actually, from the Kiwanis Club. DuPre had been very active in the Kiwanis [Club]. He had been a state officer, a regional officer, very much beloved in that organization. Mainly led by Maurice Brown, who was a former Furman Singer, I think he was president back in the early 50s…Maurice was in charge of the Kiwanis endowment. I think they gave the final gift so that it reached $10,000.

The intent was to give that award, that scholarship, to a rising senior in Furman Singers who epitomized all of the best attributes of Furman Singers: they should be a music major, they should be a vocal person, they should be a leader in Singers, etc. The intent was that the director of Furman Signers would have a strong hand in the selection of who that person was. Also in those early years, I tried to put forth in writing the criteria for that, and somehow those criteria got lost. I'm getting around to a larger picture here that's straying off the subject a little bit. At any rate, the official agreement with Furman is a very standard, "This money is set aside to award to an appropriate music student, blah blah blah." So there are virtually no details about the description of that scholarship officially on file at Furman.

As long as I was director, I was able to sort of steer the selection process toward the person I felt would be the most appropriate recipient of that. What I discovered, or what has happened, is that Furman...Because in the beginning, that award was $500 or something, which I think was the basic amount awarded, and it was understood that it was given to a student in addition to whatever scholarships they held, which made it an appropriate, not only honor, but additional money to the student.

At some point, 15 to 20 years ago, Furman began to, I don't want to use the word "insist," but they insisted that some of these endowed scholarships simply replace what money the student already had. I went round and round with Bill Thomas about his almost annually, because it applied to other scholarships as well. The Vickwell Scholarship, for instance. Carolyn Dennis, who was the first president of Singers, she has an endowed scholarship. There are other scholarships that were specifically set up for a Furman Singer, and the intent was that the monies be in addition to whatever they held so that it would be a real, positive impact.

Furman's policy was to replace money so that if one had a $10,000 scholarship and then received a $500 scholarship from DuPre Rhame, one might end up with $10,200 or something rather than $10,500, so that was sort of an ongoing battle for me with the administration. They would always go back to, well let's look at the original written agreement, and of course, none of those original agreements had this kind of detail in it. The intent of the donor was simply not reflected in that written document because it was just a straightforward, boiler plate description.

The DuPre Rhame Scholarship is still awarded, it's a part of the Spring Honors Recital awards. This happened just two weeks ago or so. And an endowed scholarship is endowed so that the scholarship will last in perpetuity. The principal monies are never touched, only the interest from that investment is awarded.

ROBERTSON: How about the Vickwell Scholarship?

VICK: It was an endowment set up by Robert J. Maxwell, Bob Maxwell, for whom the music library is named. He was a member of the choir at Westminster Presbyterian Church, and we became very good friends. He's a bachelor millionaire, never married, eccentric, has several scholarships at Furman, has a psychology scholarship, a religion scholarship, became friends with us, and every time I would bemoan the fact that we needed more scholarship dollars, pretty soon he would send me a check for $1,000 and say this should go to a worthy student.
 So he set [the Vickwell Scholarship up] as a combination of my last name, Vick, Judy [Vick's] last name Shotwell, and his last name Maxwell, so he called it the Vickwell Scholarship.

ROBERTSON: In the archival records, it's clear that you faced some difficulties in trying to perform the "Spem in alium" of Tallis. Did you ever get to perform the work?

VICK: We did it both in McCalister and at First Baptist Pickens, I think.

ROBERTSON: The Charlotte ACDA performance in 1974 – do you have any memories of that performance that stand out to you?

VICK: That performance was in Pritchard Memorial Baptist Church, which was the church I grew up in, a very large Baptist Church in downtown Charlotte. I liked the acoustics there. We did some pretty big pieces, as I recall. Bruckner, Psalm 150, and some other pretty big stuff. The convention that year was at a Holiday Inn, so the performances at the convention were confined to basically a ballroom, which is not a very good acoustical place to sing in, so I persuaded them to move our concert to this church. which was a much nicer venue and better sound and so forth. I think the Singers made a very strong impression on the convention, because very few choirs were doing that kind of literature, that big of literature, and the Singers sang wonderfully.

Interview, Bingham Vick, Jr., May 9, 2011

ROBERTSON: Do you have any personal memories of the Romania trip that stand out?

VICK: Romania was a real learning experience. That was the first trip that I had taken Furman Singers on, that Judy and I had taken. Any time you have a first experience at something…We had toured the United States, and that's one thing, but travelling in a foreign country at that time, this was 1974…Just making sure all the arrangements for air travel, etc. was a whole new kind of ball game. When we got there, we had been assured that because it was a sixteen hour flight, we were dead on our feet when we got into Bucharest at like six in the morning after a day and a half of flying in a cramped airplane.

We arrived, and when we got off the plane there were guards standing around with submachine guns in their hands. This was a Communist country; everything was very controlled. They insisted on going through lots of bags. Customs officials can be sort of power play people; they do things to you because they can. We get to the hotel at like nine o'clock or 9:30 and the rooms aren't ready. All we want to do is take a shower and take a nap. Stretch out in a bed. So we have to wander around for about an hour and a half, and it's like 90 degrees in Bucharest.

We finally get checked into the hotel and, of course, everybody wants to go take a shower because you just feel grungy. Well, the hotel decided we were using too much water, so they just shut off the water. I mean, cut it off. Not the hot water – the water. So if you were lathered up in the shower and the water goes off, you're stuck. We discovered later, after complaining through our interpreters and so forth that they thought we were using too much hot water, so they just shut it off. That was sort of our introduction to Communist-controlled Romania. You do exactly what they want you to when they say do it, or there will be some consequences.

We finally got to lunch at about one o'clock, and on this trip we had breakfast and lunch and dinner always provided. Lunch and dinner were always big, hot meals, starting with a bowl of hot soup. Very few things are air conditioned – did I mention it was 95 degrees or something? So we're excited about being there, we're tired, we go through this rigmarole at the hotel. These were new experiences for me as a young conductor, and for me as somebody in charge of an ensemble. I'm used to going to the front desk and fixing something. Here it just didn't happen, so there was a level of frustration there.

We had a restful afternoon, had supper at like five o'clock. They told us we would not sing for a couple of days so that we could get acclimated. As we were at five o'clock eating our second hot meal of the day word came that we were giving a concert at seven o'clock, our first concert. We had been through this hassle arriving, hassle at the hotel, we were hot, we were not well rested, and then we were informed that in an hour-and-a-half we were giving our first concert, which was a very exciting thing. There were a lot of mixed emotions. You're excited about doing the concert, but you're tired and you're hot. All that was new for me. It's not like travelling in the United States where I pretty much knew how much time it was going to take and how much rest we would have and so forth.

The first concert went great. We had, I think, two kids faint, because there were 105 of us, which means three buses. Frequently on that trip we were in two hotels or three hotels; nobody in Romania spoke English. That was disconcerting for me to know that a third of my children are somewhere, and I have no idea where, and if I had to get in touch with them, it would be a real hassle. There are some real issues there, just technical, day-to-day travelling issues that were new to me.

The concert went great. This is still seared into my mind: following the concert they said, we want you all to come over here to this sort of fellowship room and we went in, and here were big tubs of iced Pepsis. This was before Pepsis in cans, so these were iced tubs of bottles of Pepsi, and we all thought we had died and gone to heaven right there.

That whole trip was incredible. We had great concerts; the kids sang well. We had taken little American flags to give out at the end of the concert and no sooner on our last number, I think our last number was, "I'd Like to Teach the World to Sing," that was the big commercial song at the time. The young people in the audience would rush the stage to get a flag. For them that was an incredible treat.

We travelled all over Romania; we had a wonderful experience. It was constant adjusting, adapting, and accepting. We would stop and get ready to check in some place and our guide would go in, and I would go in with them, and the guide and the hotel person would have this very animated conversation sort of yelling back and forth and gesturing and all this sort of thing. Then the guide would turn to me and say, everything's ok. That's the way they communicate – they yell at each other.

So it was a great experience. It was difficult because there were three busloads of us, and everything was new. I think, especially, being there when Nixon resigned was a real eye-opening experience for the students because the guides over there…One of our guides said, aren't you worried your country will be in turmoil and there'll be rioting and there'll be martial law? We said no, the vice president will take over. Because, in those countries, if something happened, all hell would break loose, and there would be no law, and it would be pandemonium. So, for them to see that we have an orderly transition of leadership…

Some of the people we met would say things to me in conversation like, why would you not want Nixon as president? He was such a good president; he did so much good for the country in terms of relations with Europe, etc., etc. My response was generally, well he may have been a good president for America with Europe, but he wasn't a good president for America at home because of the way he did things. And that was sort of the way he was known at the time. He was a great foreign policy facilitator, but he really got himself in deep stuff at home.

ROBERTSON: Talk for a bit about the concept "Adjust, adapt, accept." When did that become a mantra for Furman Singers tour?

VICK: I don't know exactly when. A friend of ours, Robert J. Maxwell, who was very generous to Furman and who became very good friends with us, back in the late 50s he went through a real issue with alcohol and put himself in a rehab treatment center, etc. One of the things he would always say to me was that he learned there, through his counselor to adjust, adapt, and accept. You don't use alcohol to wash away the problem. You don't use alcohol to cover up a problem; you don't use alcohol to try to deal with a problem. The mantra of adjust, adapt, and accept, he really told me that was the way he was counseled to get through his dealings with alcohol.

And certainly before this trip, and whether we had it before this trip or after this trip, it just made sense in a big way. The more I thought about it, that really is a life's lesson. In life things are not going to go the way you want. You can fight against them, you can get all upset, you can abuse your body, you can abuse other people, but that will not necessarily change the situation. In touring, and particularly in Romania, because almost everything that we had been told up front in terms of schedule, in terms of how this would happen, how that would happen, almost everything was different when we got there. For me, being someone who, when I went on tour, wanted to know we were going to be on the road for an hour and a half and we would arrive exactly at 4:30 and we would have this much time to this…I thought it important to have a good idea of those details in order that the whole trip, tour, went well and we had enough time to do this and enough time to do that.

So over there, nothing was that way, and often we were rushed, often we had to wait. The schedule we had been given up front was not the schedule that we actually followed when we got there. That's just the way they did things was the response. I had to do a lot of mental adjustment myself. If I get upset in front of the ensemble, then they're reading me. For the good of the ensemble I had to figure out a way to make the best of it, to complain when I thought I could get some response, but to know when to back off and say, ok, it's gonna be that way; let's just deal with it.

That's one of several things that I think sort of helped my work with Singers and helped Singers as you dealt with whatever at Furman or with Furman Singers or on tour or what have you. As a conductor, I'm getting to that point with the Beethoven [*Missa Solemnis*] in these next two weeks. I know every time they make a mistake, the chorus, in rehearsals. There is not time to stop and fix every little thing. I've tried to put as much responsibility on them to practice outside, to do the work on their own; there are computer programs, there's a computer program, you can go, and it will play you the bass part in the *Missa Solemnis* slowly, at tempo, with orchestra...There are just a lot of helps, and I've encouraged them to do that. So, I'm getting to that point with the Beethoven.

As a conductor I find myself doing that all the time. You're deciding is it worth rehearsal time to stop and fix this? Maybe it'll fix itself. If it doesn't fix itself, can I live with that? The closer you get to a concert, the more you're looking at the big picture. I've planned rehearsals very carefully, but I'm to the point where I know tonight, before we get there, there are gonna be some places that are just not right. So I've got to figure, do I accept it and move on, do I stop and make some adjustment somehow?

ROBERTSON: What was different by the time of the Moscow tour? By then you had done several European tours.

VICK: After Romania, and then we went to England the next year, where things were pretty much the way we were told they would be, so that my mindset was, this is the schedule that I've worked out with them, this is how much free time, this is when we'll perform, when we'll need to do this, that, and the other. For several trips that was the norm, and it didn't matter whether it was England or Germany. If it was in Italy, then you just had to understand that Italian time is different. If they say seven o'clock they mean, somewhere around seven o'clock. It might be 7:30. So you just sort of adjust to that.

Our first trip to Russia was returning to, at that time, a Communist country, so we knew everything was going to be much more controlled. Our access to certain areas would be restricted, much like Romania. As it turned out, we never felt that restriction. Everything was pretty much according to the plan that had been given to us up front. The day that we sang in the Cathedral of the Assumption, as I said, we were scheduled to sing in Gorky Park, which is an outdoor venue, but it was really pouring rain, and when we called the park they said the concert's canceled. There's nobody here; it's pouring rain; you couldn't do it anyway. So that was really a serendipitous possibility to go back and sing at this cathedral.

Other than that, by that time…We started in '74. By '91 we had been on enough of these trips that I pretty much knew what to expect. I knew what could go wrong, what probably would go wrong, what most likely would be fine. That really wasn't much of an adjustment.

ROBERTSON: You wrote a few sentences about the night of the first Boston Pops performance – could you talk about that for a minute?

VICK: Keith [Lockhart, Furman University alumnus and conductor of the Boston Pops] had visited Furman in February of '96. He had just been appointed that fall the conductor of the Boston Pops. He was here; we had a luncheon; I was chatting with him at lunch and I said, "Furman Singers would love to sing with you guys" just by way of conversation. He sort of got a funny look on his face and he said, "Well, what about this summer?" That sort of took me aback, and I said, "Great!" He said, "Well, let's talk about this. Since I was just appointed new conductor, nobody made arrangements for a chorus for the summer Fourth of July concert. Normally they use Tanglewood's chorus or they have some other groups in the Boston area. Because of the change of conductors nobody had hired a chorus."

That was sort of the start of that project, and over a period of weeks it worked out that yes, they wanted us. They could put as many as 75 on the stage. I had to decide who could go. It was sort of, who can go? Then in order to get a balanced ensemble we had some extra rehearsals and you've gotta come back to Furman, so I had to make arrangements for overnight housing for a night, right before we left. Furman stepped up to pay for…Because we paid our own way, the Pops didn't pay for anything. Martha Vaughn, who was working in administration at that time made all the arrangements for us. She talked to the hotels up there; she talked to Eastern Airlines or whoever we flew with. We had to go up on two flights.

We stayed at a great hotel right downtown next to the Harvard Club, a really fine sort of…the rooms were all suites. They had a living room and then a separate bedroom and so forth. Very convenient to Orchestra Hall where we rehearsed. We got there on a Sunday night. We had a Monday afternoon piano rehearsal with Keith at Orchestra Hall, supper; Monday night was orchestra rehearsal in the hall. Tuesday afternoon they do a dress rehearsal at the park, which only has maybe 200,000 people show up, because it's the whole show, but because it's televised, they have to practice the camera angles and the timing and all that sort of stuff.

Tuesday afternoon we went to the park and did the run through, sort of a dress rehearsal. Wednesday night was the Fourth of July and we were to sing. It rained all day on Wednesday. It was raining when we were supposed to start the concert at eight o'clock, so they had to delay that because the instruments couldn't play out in the rain. Then [Lockhart] had to shorten the concert on the fly while we got started. It was just a phenomenal evening.

Keith's assistant, Dennis Alves...We had the feeling that, because of the other choruses they had used, Dennis Alves, who didn't know us, thought, ok, Keith's invited his college choir to come up and sing. This is gonna be sort of minimally acceptable. At the very first piano rehearsal, Keith was conducting, of course, and I don't even remember what the first thing we did was, but the Singers just knocked their socks of and sounded great and followed Keith to the Nth degree, and Keith did about half the number and stopped and turned to Dennis and said, "Didn't I tell you they were good?"

The relationship with the Pops was great. In the rehearsals they were very friendly, supportive. We had a very good rapport with the individual players, and Keith really enjoyed working with the Singers. They were very well prepared. When we got to the stage and had to do some stage adjustment in terms of how to put people where, you know, Singers were accustomed to being pushed around on stage because when we go on tour we have to finagle ourselves into a choir loft that doesn't fit us. They were accustomed to that. It was just a super experience.

ROBERTSON: Talk for a moment about your recollections of that night, at the concert.

VICK: The Pops, as we learned from that experience and the two Christmas things...First of all, they are a truly outstanding professional orchestra. They play phenomenally well, but even if it's Pops music, they play it really, really well. All of these players are superb musicians. The concert in the park is like a giant party for everybody. The players enjoy it, the 400,000 people who are there enjoy it, the 200,000 who are right in front of the stage love every minute of it. It's a great television production; it's fun to watch it on TV. They've done it for so many years and so successfully that I think the whole Boston, New England community looks forward to that evening.

It's a no-alcohol situation. There's never any rowdiness or fighting or any hint of any disruption. The fireworks display over the river is just beyond description, about 35 or 40 minutes of just the most spectacular stuff you can ever imagine. And then following that concert, because after the concert they said, if you want to go back to the hotel, the buses will leave right after the concert, before the fireworks. A lot of the orchestra, they've done it every year. They don't care to stay. So the buses leave and take them back. Because of the size of the crowds they have to shut down all the roads around the park area. So there is no traffic, because there's no place for traffic to be with that many people. And what we wound up doing was walking back to our hotel, which was about 12 blocks, in this mass of humanity, all of whom were just walking together and singing the patriotic songs that they'd just heard, and just having a grand old time. It was like being in a fabulous party, and you didn't know any of these people, but everybody was having a great time.

That's almost an unbelievable kind of experience, unless you've been there. It's like if the entire population of Greenville had a party downtown and everyone walked down Poinsett Highway. Because you're talking about a four, six lane road, full of people, meandering along, singing, having a good time, at 11 o'clock at night. And the Singers were just great, they sang well, they behaved themselves. When we checked out of the hotel, the manager of the hotel said, not only did we as a staff enjoy having your students here, but some of the other guests in the hotel said how much they had enjoyed having your students with us. How many groups of 75 college students coming into a hotel would that happen with? Which speaks, I think, to the discipline of Singers, and surely what I don't know won't hurt me.

ROBERTSON: Talk for a moment about the fundraising effort for Harper Hall.

VICK: When [Dave] Vassy called me and said, the 50th anniversary is coming up and we want to do something special, I said immediately, we need a rehearsal space. How much money are you talking about raising, because that's what we really need. To make a long story short, he put together a committee, worked with the development office, developed a plan, went out and did it. The Singers response was phenomenal. There were some major gifts from non-Singers involved in there, which is the way you do things when you're raising that kind of money.

ROBERTSON: Were the Harpers not Singers?

VICK: No. They were good friends of Furman, and Don Lineback persuaded them to give a substantial naming gift. He had talked to Gordon and Sarah about their gift, and there were some natural confluences that happened. Furman Singers, "Brown Eyes" being the Furman song, Nan Trammell Herring being Gordon's mother, who brought that song to Furman, the Herrings' generosity in general, they were both Furman Singers. So it was really Don who encouraged them and they stepped up significantly to make that happen.

ROBERTSON: How about the day of the dedication?

VICK: The day of the dedication was…As you know I get emotional easily, and to see something like that actually come to fruition was just phenomenally moving. Then Aubrey and Becky Daniels commissioned David Schwoebel, all of that unbeknownst to me until the last minute, to write a piece for the dedication. That little benediction that he wrote, "Father Give Thy Benediction," was sort of just the icing on the cake.

All of the major donors had been invited; most of them came. It was a really grand celebration. What started as just a rehearsal room really produced a music library, a music seminar room that's equipped to the hilt with the latest technology, a computer lab as a part of the music library. Plus, the rehearsal room is not just for Furman Singers, it's audio-visually stocked; it's used during the day for a myriad of classes. We can put orchestra and chorus in there; it can be used as a recital space.

ROBERTSON: Did you know Nan Trammell Herring?

VICK: I did not. Singers sang for her funeral. Most of them didn't really understand why. It was a very humble funeral at a Baptist church out on Lee Road. It was not a big Baptist church, high-powered sort of thing. It was a very wonderful and moving service. We were happy to be able to do that.

ROBERTSON: Could you talk about your impressions of the 2009 Singers reunion?

VICK: It was pretty overwhelming. Musically it was a phenomenal worship experience. I still have people come up to me, miscellaneous people, not Furman Singers, people who are members of First Baptist or who went that Sunday, to say they were so moved with the beauty of the music. Not only was it a huge ensemble, which is impressive to start with, but I think the recording shows, and certainly my experience was, that just the pure excellence and beauty of the music that was performed was a phenomenal experience in and of itself. And certainly the spirit of everybody there…

When I look at a group of Furman Singers last year, and you know this if you've been in an ensemble, if you've been with the ensemble for any length of time, you're not seeing Suzy the soprano, you're seeing Suzy the soprano from Timbuktu whose brother has cancer and whose mother is divorced. You have all these personal, related thoughts and memories. With the Singers reunion, that's multiplied by 350. I look around and everywhere I look, there's somebody with some interesting, important, meaningful, emotional story attached to that person.

I look at you, I see your brother, I see your parents, I see Bell Tower Boys, I see all of these things that you did when you were at Furman, all wrapped into that one, instantaneous vision. With so many of the Singers that was my experience, standing there and making music. Knowing my emotionality, dirty socks didn't cut it. Going in I knew I was going to have to…You know I wanted to enjoy the moment, and I didn't want to deny the emotional aspect, but I also knew that I had to find some way to keep it together in spite of all of those personal memories and so forth.

It was a real…it was an emotional day.

ROBERTSON: The *Mass in B Minor Concert*, what impressions do you have of that experience?

VICK: That was an emotional day. I had planned retirement several years in advance because I knew the rotation of conductors. I knew there were some things I wanted to do with Furman Singers, so for the last four or five or six years, for tour, my tour repertoire was basically stuff I really loved doing. I wanted to do, one more time, Stanford's "Beati" and "Canticle of Invocation." Some of these things that, for me, Singers had always done so well, and they had such a good sound doing it.

In planning, I knew when my last rotation to do *Messiah* would be. I decided early on we'll do the whole thing. We'd never done the whole thing. We'd done Part I and Part II, or I and III, or we'd done excerpts. So for the first time at Furman we did the entire *Messiah*, which I think every musician ought to do at least once in their life. Handel put that piece together as a whole. He didn't put it together to be chopped up. We learned to do that after the fact. It takes a long time, it takes an audience willing to be there for that long, and we're accustomed to hour, hour-and-a-half concerts, not two-and-a-half-hour concerts. There was…I realized there would be some adjustment, but I felt like it was worth the effort to do that.

For me, personally, I think that the *B Minor* is the greatest piece of music ever written. Singers had never done it; we had done some excerpts from it. I wanted that to be my last hurrah, as it were.

Tom Joiner was very supportive in the whole process, and he said early on, let's make this a festival orchestra, i.e. include faculty members; to make sure we had an absolutely superb horn player, we had a faculty horn player. He wanted to play first violin, because there were a couple of solo parts that were really just phenomenally difficult to play. He wanted Gary Malvern playing trumpet if possible. So he was able to pull together a student and faculty orchestra that was really superb.

I felt like we had student soloists who could do everything and they did. We've always had great sopranos, we've had good mezzos, we've had outstanding basses, baritones, and tenors. The "Benedictus" movement for tenor is very, very hard to do. I think our students did very well. I was very pleased with the soloists, with the chorus, with the orchestra. It certainly was a personal, professional highlight of my life to do that work there.

Interview, Bingham Vick, Jr., June 6, 2011

ROBERTSON: Talk for a moment about the situation of Furman Singers and Concert Choir as parallel ensembles.

VICK: Both of the groups were auditioned, and in some cases, the students would audition for both. They would not really have been accepted into Singers but they were accepted into Choir, so it wasn't a matter of the standards being higher, but it made for a very awkward situation, needless to say. Milburn and I got along fine. Once we got past the beginning of the year and the recruiting issues, then we each understood whose turf was whose, and everything was fine.

When Milburn left in 1981 to go to Southern Seminary, it was an obvious time to stop Concert Choir touring, to just sort of combine Concert Choir and Furman Singers. In terms of personnel, I had already had Chamber Singers going, starting in the early 1970s as a small ensemble to do vocal chamber music and the PDQ Bach stuff and so forth. There was actually a third chorus paralleling all this, University Chorus, which was basically a come one, come all sort of thing. When Concert Choir folded, we started the University Chorus, and I conducted University Chorus and Singers for four or five years, I think. At that time there were plenty of personnel. We had anywhere from 80 to 100 in Chorus, and I had close to 100 in Singers. Chorus was obviously non-auditioned.

ROBERTSON: Milburn Price decided to leave for the seminary on his own?

VICK: Oh yeah. His decision to go to Southern was made during a time when conservative Southern Baptists were putting a lot of pressure all over the Southern Baptist Convention on various institutions. Milburn already had a fine reputation as a church musician, so he left to become the dean of the School of Music at the Southern Seminary because he felt he could really make a difference, uphold standards, and deal with the Baptists, and so on. He did that very well for about ten years and then it got too much for him, so he left and went to Samford. His move was his own, professional decision.

ROBERTSON: What were the Furman Singers conversations about ensemble size like?

VICK: When I came to Furman in 1970, Singers had 85 or so. Then I sort of inherited…Singers was not exclusively selective. The numbers grew each year; there were already a number of people in Singers who I didn't want to kick out. By the mid-1970s it got to pretty obnoxious numbers, like 200. At that point, purchasing music was an issue; rehearsal space was an issue. It was a matter of, we have all these people who want to sing, but there's no choir for them to be in. I started paring back in terms of being more selective; I got the group down to around 125. Especially by the end of the 1970s I had University Chorus and that took all of the overflow.

By the late 1980s I pulled it, through auditions, back down to 100 or so. That would vary depending on voice parts.

ROBERTSON: Talk a bit about DuPre Rhame in terms of his persona.

VICK: He was a very strong personality. He had been teaching at Furman for 20 years or so with Furman Singers. Over that time he had developed a strong position in terms of the fine arts. I think he was the head of the fine arts division. He did *Messiah* every year with a separate budget line. At Furman, a lot of power is associated with who has control over what budget, and he had developed not only a Singers budget but also a *Messiah* line, just specifically for *Messiah*.

He was highly regarded across the campus with other faculty. Some people really respected him; some people did not because he tended to get his way if there were issues. There was conflict with the drama department, for instance. At that point we didn't have the music building, so everyone had to share McAlister. DuPre had a reputation for throwing his weight around to get rehearsal space. As with any powerful personality, I think people either tended to like him or not.

His relationship with me was always very good. He invited me to join the Greenville Kiwanis Club, so every two weeks we would go to Kiwanis, spend good, quality time. He was a very kind and thoughtful person. He kept a hands-off approach when I came in, other than our disagreement about soloists for *Messiah*. That was about the only difference of opinion we had, and he respected me enough to not pursue it.

He would always send me a note before tour and after the home concert. He was very supportive. He had been trained in New York, before music people really got doctorates. He had studied beyond the master's degree. He had a beautiful, deep baritone voice. Did a lot of solo work, taught voice. He was very highly regarded on the music faculty. He was a great guy: a gentleman, a southern gentleman.

Interview, Gordon and Sarah Herring, May 9, 2011

GORDON: Mother was born in 1907 and her parents moved to Greenville, where she spent the rest of her youth. She, like her mother, attended Greenville Woman's College. That was before, obviously, it became a part of Furman. She graduated in 1929 and then went from Furman to Cornell and got a master's degree in English, which was fairly uncommon for a young lady in those days.

While she was at Furman…She had a beautiful voice, a beautiful soprano voice, and she was called upon to sing at various fraternity parties and various events and so forth. As a child she would visit with her aunt, Mary Fanny Lanier, who lived in West Point, Georgia. This is kind of an aside, but Mary Fanny was very proud of the fact that her husband was related to Sydney Lanier, the poet. But when Mother would spend some time with Mary Fanny, she would learn a lot of folk songs because Mary Fanny was also very musically inclined. She played the organ at her church. There were a number of songs that Mother learned as a child, one of them being "Brown Eyes." She, when she was at Furman, and was asked to sing at fraternity parties and what have you, "Brown Eyes" typically was one of the ones that she would sing. I remember, long after her graduation from Furman, her singing that to me.

Probably the time when "Brown Eyes" finally became committed…It was never composed, never written down. The leader of the pep band wanted for Mother to sing it at a basketball game, so he called her on the phone. She sang it, note by note, and he wrote it down and then composed the first version, the first iteration of it. They played it for a basketball game, and that was perhaps one of the first public performances. Later, DuPre Rhame did an arrangement, which is the one that they're doing now. Mother never really understood why one of the many, many songs that she learned as a child became so popular, but it kind of took on a life of its own.

ROBERTSON: Do you think that had anything to do with her personality or her friends' regard for her?

GORDON: Perhaps it did, but it was one of a number of songs that she sang. She sang it beautifully, and it still kind of tugs at my heart when I hear it.

She graduated from Cornell with a master's degree in English. My father had also attended Furman. He didn't graduate, but he was also in the class of '29. He went to dental school for a brief period and then felt the call to the ministry and he and Mother were married. They went to the seminary and they had a pastorate in Jackson, Mississippi, briefly.

There was a couple in China. The wife had a nervous breakdown and they had to come home, so they needed a quick replacement for them, and because Dad had been born in China and spoke Chinese before he spoke English, they appointed them as missionaries and they went directly to the field, and Mother never got a chance to have language school. She was trying to catch up with learning the language while they were actually on location. One of the things that they always said about Mother was that she spoke Chinese with a South Carolinian accent.

ROBERTSON: So your father was the son of missionaries?

GORDON: Yeah, Dad was born in China in 1905. His parents went to China in 1885. Mother and Dad retired from the mission field in 1969 and came back to Greenville.

SARAH: Part of the appeal of "Brown Eyes" was that it was a ballad, a love song, and it was used to serenade.

GORDON: The fraternities picked it up…

SARAH: They socialized it to where it became sort of a theme, "Brown Eyes, good night."

GORDON: And DuPre wrote the arrangement they use today. Almost every concert of the Furman Singers dating back to early DuPre times, every concert he performed it. He had a major role in making that part of the fabric of Furman.

ROBERTSON: What was it like to be her son, performing her song in Furman Singers?

GORDON: At the time it was really not a whole lot of comment about it. It was interesting how many people claimed to have written "Brown Eyes." I know there was one woman who claimed that her husband wrote it for her and that she was the subject. There were a number of these kinds of stories going around, and that was primarily why Gordon Blackwell wrote the history of it that he did, to clarify and document that. There were a number of interesting stories about people claiming to be the subject of "Brown Eyes."

SARAH: When you were at Furman, did you associate "Brown Eyes" with your mother then? I didn't know the connection.

GORDON: Oh, yeah. At that time there was not a whole lot of discussion about where it came from or anything. It was more in the Gordon Blackwell era. And a lot of it was because of all the lore that was coming up around…And he knew Mother. He was younger than Mother, but he knew my parents. I never talked to him about why he wrote it or what he did, but I'm pretty sure it was to set the record straight.

ROBERTSON: Do you have any memories that you would like to share?

GORDON: Just that our tours were bus tours through the close-by states of the southeast.

SARAH: We'd be doing the big town of Washington, North Carolina, and that would be one of the hot spots.

GORDON: The Singers during that time didn't do any international touring, for sure, and we didn't get too far from South Carolina.

SARAH: One of the tours went to Virginia.

GORDON: They were all bus trips, and we as managers had to get all the robes crammed into heavy wooden boxes.

SARAH: In those days the women wore formals that they provided themselves for tours, and in the 60s the fashion was that you had multiple slips and petticoats. You couldn't get as many people on the riser with all their formal dresses on as you could when you had everybody crammed in robes. And that became a challenge for the managers to make sure that we could place everybody because not only the packing was a hassle, but all of these skirts had to have multiple ruffles and multiple… I think we were past the hoop time, but there were some tours that the hoops were in, which would have really been hard.

You had your formal that you got out to put on every night and it really started to be ramshackle by the end of tour. But we would wear robes for the sacred part of the tour and then take off robes and then be in the looking more faded formals by the end of the week.

GORDON: DuPre would have turned over in his grave, though, for the less formal part under Bing. That would have been difficult for DuPre to have been involved in, but Bing made it fun; he lightened the…Especially after a very serious, religious section of the concert, Bing brought a little life to it. But it was more the formal petticoats in DuPre's day.

GORDON: A lot of the concerts were for civic groups. We would go to the Poinsett Hotel and sing in that beautiful Gold Room, which wasn't so beautiful at the time, for a number of civic groups that the Singers would perform for. It was much more of a local flavor. Rehearsals were in McAllister Auditorium.

SARAH: We practiced on Tuesdays and Thursdays, and we sang for chapel on those days. The Tuesday program was secular, informational, but the Thursday program was actually a chapel service. It was mandatory, not just for Singers but for all the students. The seat checker would sit up in the balcony…

GORDON: You had to sit in an assigned seat, and they would check the empty seats and see who didn't make it to chapel.

SARAH: And so you couldn't graduate if you had missed too many times at chapel. You had a very limited number of cuts from chapel.

ROBERTSON: Do you have any recollections of the staged music DuPre Rhame enjoyed?

SARAH: We did *Faust*…

GORDON: *Carmen*…

SARAH: I think those were my two. I don't think we did something every year.

GORDON: It was every other year, and DuPre would bring in professional soloists.

SARAH: But he would have understudies in the Singers who did the solo parts up until the professionals showed up. We rented costumes, and apparently there was a pretty big budget for the deal, relatively speaking. Of course the costumes were not the greatest thing in the world, but everybody got a costume, because we were the traditional orchestra chorus. Most everybody did participate, but….

GORDON: Yeah, this wasn't mandatory, but the choruses were big. The music majors sang in the Concert Choir, and very few of them sang in the Singers. Jerry Langenkamp led the Concert Choir, and that was the equivalent of the one that Bill Thomas does now. But now a lot of those kids sing in both the Singers and Chamber Choir.

ROBERTSON: So the Concert Choir at that time was mostly music majors?

GORDON: Yes, they were music majors and vocal performance.

SARAH: And they couldn't, because of rehearsal conflicts, be in Singers as much as anything. The vocal…

GORDON: The trained voices typically sang in Concert Choir.

ROBERTSON: Did either of you participate in the productions?

GORDON: We were in the operas, yeah.

SARAH: Not as solo voices, but we were always the background, the dancers. I was actually, I danced in *Carmen*. I was one of the gypsy dancers. *Faust* required a lot of background, gesticulating and things. We worked hard in both of them, because there was a lot of production happening with the scenery and getting all the costuming coordinated. It was a major thing for us. We did that in the spring each year.

GORDON: One thing I remember about it: I had helped a little with the set, and the drama department produced those. I forget the professor's name, but it was a scene with a forest, and in between acts he realized that we had not trimmed the canvas to make it look like leaves, and so we lowered that part and we were there cutting away at the canvas to keep it from looking like just a straight line…

SARAH: I think that was in *Carmen* when the gypsies are hiding away…

GORDON: It extended the intermission a lot longer than DuPre was happy with…

ROBERTSON: During the production?

GORDON: Oh yeah, during the production.

SARAH: It was not the most professional of presentations but our hearts were in the right place. Did we do it twice? We did it twice, I think.

GORDON: I think it was just once, because all the soloists came down from New York.

SARAH: I bet we did it two nights in a row, maybe not…

ROBERTSON: It seems remarkable that he would fly in soloists from New York.

GORDON: Oh, it was the big event of the year, the headline of the entire music program.

SARAH: Because there was no student production.

Interview, James E. Williams, III, June 1, 2011

ROBERTSON: Talk for a moment about your recollections of Singers.

WILLIAMS: Some of my fondest musical memories to date happened under Dr. Vick's direction. The places we would tour, the music we would sing are things that have stuck with me. I continue to try to emulate him in my conducting and in my pursuits as a choral director. He was always a very clear and precise conductor, a very personable director, someone you could always go to and rely on for advice, a great father figure to many people. He was that to me in musical and other senses, somebody I admire and continue to appreciate more, as I get into my career, and the influence he had on me and many others through Furman Singers.

ROBERTSON: What was it like to be a student conductor?

WILLIAMS: I was very fortunate to share that responsibility with Ginny Carroll. The both of us got a great experience through that, to be in front of your peers as a senior in college, one who's aiming to be a music educator and conductor. To have that experience with him as your mentor…he was never a person who would call you out in rehearsal on a gesture or pacing or whatnot. It was one of those things where he knew the perfect time to comment on things and to nurture you and continue with you, whether it was outside of rehearsal, before rehearsal, or in a classroom setting. He just had a way of demonstrating his own conducting and how he would go through a passage, but also give you the liberty to make decisions for yourself.

The piece that I was able to do, the Casals "O Vos Omnes," was a pretty large, 16-part piece that I taught the group. It's not very common that you're able to work with such a fine ensemble at a young age. To have that experience and that opportunity with him as your mentor was pretty remarkable.

ROBERTSON: What about being president and an officer?

WILLIAMS: I recall very informal but relevant discussions with him and the other officers. I remember meeting at his house to talk about plans for social events for engaging the new Singers, the freshman class. Planning out the picnic. I remember that being a cool responsibility. Giving people the opportunity to make a really unique ensemble experience was great. He was very hands-off in many ways.

He wanted the president and others to have ownership. I don't remember him vetoing or strongly wording anything he wanted us to do, but I remember him being the voice of reason as well. He knew from his years of directing experience what things worked and what didn't. From a managerial side of things it was a cool experience as well. Of course he had the musical side as leadership, but to see how you could work outside rehearsal and building *esprit de corps* and ensemble was great.

ROBERTSON: What about Mosquitoes?

WILLIAMS: I remember that just being fun. It was never…it didn't ever seem like work. Dr. Vick would run rehearsals and we would have a great time doing it. It never felt like he was a slave driver or a task master. We all had common goals, and it was, obviously, a unique experience to be able to sing with your mentor in such a fun style.

I have fond memories of going on tour, the kind of reception that barber shop would get. We would sing for civic groups and I remember that being very unique because of the style difference.

ROBERTSON: So Dr. Vick was more relaxed than in Furman Singers?

WILLIAMS: I would say so, because it's not necessarily a style of music that you have to be so musically…It's more of a musical theater sort of quality. He would want to make sure we were taking care of details, but have a good time and take care of the showmanship side of it, too. It wasn't as strict. The pacing of rehearsals was very loose. We would always get the job done, and he knew how to do it.

ROBERTSON: Do you have any specific memory you would like to share?

WILLIAMS: One of my most significant memories was that, on the last European tour I was able to share…It was after my graduation, and we were on our last concert in Nürnberg. Dr. Vick asked me if there was something on the program I'd like to conduct. I'm actually staring at the picture of the church. I have it in my office here. He asked me what I wanted to do, and there were so many great things on the program, but it was the Lauridsen "O Magnum Mysterium" because of the ethereal nature of it and the environment we were able to sing in. Him having that kind of confidence in me, turning over something that he had never seen me conduct before, that he felt that I was capable and ready for such a task… That confidence that he had in me was probably the most flattering. Then, of course, the musical side of things when we actually performed the piece. The expressions on the faces of those who were singing and just their common goal in making music, whether it be for me or Dr. Vick. It was an awesome thing for me, and that was how I capped off my musical experience with Furman Singers. It's something I'll never forget.

Interview, Carolyn Dennis, June 2, 2011

ROBERTSON: I noticed that there is no overlap in the personnel of the Serenaders – could you talk about the formation of that group and its makeup?

DENNIS: I started Furman in 1943, at 16 years of age, very young. We only had 11 grades in high school then. It was right in the middle of World War II. Mr. Rhame had always a male glee club, and of course, the war took care of that for him. All the boys were gone.
    There were a few of us who were studying with Mr. Rhame, and we said, can't we just do some three-part harmony or something?

So we developed this choral group called the Serenaders. We did a few things that small groups could do. We sang for the troops in the USO Building downtown, and (Mr. Rhame was a great Kiwanian) we sang often for the Kiwanis Club, and any other thing that he was asked to have a group to do, the Serenaders did it for him. It was a very pleasant group, small, but we made pretty good music.

ROBERTSON: You were all Mr. Rhame's voice students?

DENNIS: Yes, well...we weren't all voice students. I guess most of us were. I know Ellen Bridges was the pianist. She was a piano major. Everybody was in the music department. Everybody in the Serenaders was in some part of the music department.

The meeting to determine what would happen with that came in 1946. The war was over in 1945, and the boys started coming back in second semester of 1945. They had part of that year, and then in 1946 all of them were back that were coming back. Of course, Mr. Rhame, I'm sure the thought had entered his mind that he would go back and have his male glee club again, but we had gotten so close to him, and I in particular.

Mr. Rhame was a very close, personal friend of mine, and his family. Peetsie Gulledge, his older child, and I were very good friends. An interesting aside to that is that one of Peetsie's daughters is a best friend, starting in second grade until today. But, anyway, Mr. Rhame, I had a very special relationship with him. So some of us went to him and said, you know, don't throw us out with the bathwater please. Let the girls sing along with the boys. That's when the idea of having a group...

We met in the fall of 1946, at the beginning of the first semester, 1946. We met in the old chapel on the men's campus to determine our future. That day, he had already decided that he would have a mixed chorus. We met that day and a few names were tossed around. The Serenaders, of course, which we had been before, that was considered. Somebody suggested the Furman Singers, which went over great. From that day on, we became the Furman Singers.

ROBERTSON: And you were elected the first president of Furman Singers.

DENNIS: I was elected the first president of the Singers, yes. And still here to talk about it! In spring of 1947 we did *The Gondoliers*, and I did my graduating recital and had a leading role in the operetta. That was a very busy semester for me.

ROBERTSON: As president, what sorts of things did Mr. Rhame have you do?

DENNIS: Just the usual things that presidents do. Try to make sure you talked to everybody…of course we didn't have much problem. Everybody was so glad to be back, the boys especially. There was a camaraderie in that group, and it's amazing, because it's still there today. It's gone through every generation. It was an easy job for me. I didn't have much to do with it. I think it was more popularity contest than anything else.

ROBERTSON: Could you talk for just a moment about Mr. Rhame as a conductor as well as your personal experiences with him?

DENNIS: My personal experiences with him were very special. Of course, I took voice lessons and Mrs. Rhame always played for my lessons. It was a challenging time, and I loved opera and so did Mr.

Rhame. I did an awful lot of arias from operas. For my graduating recital I sang Mimi's aria from *La Boheme,* and also a Verdi aria from *La Traviata.* So you can tell that it was not just basic songs. I had a great recital, it was wonderful. It was what I loved and what he loved.

Studying with him was just very special for me. When he was directing he had a way of just pulling you with him. My husband always said to me that if Mr. Rhame asked me to walk on the water, I would try. It was just a wonderful relationship. As I told you before because we were so close as family friends, the day I was married, when my husband and I flew to New York City, the first time I had been to New York City and my first trip to the Metropolitan Opera, Mr. and Mrs. Rhame and Peetsie all were at the airport to see us leave. It was just more like family than teacher and student.

ROBERTSON: Do you have any outstanding memories of that time that you would want to share?

DENNIS: Well, there are two female leads in *The Gondoliers.* One of them is the beautiful girl, the queen or something, and she only sings once. When Mr. Rhame came to me and said, "Now Carolyn, you have two choices, and you have first choice." I said, "Which one has the most singing to do?" It was the other role, so I chose that one. I didn't care anything about it being the queen.
It was an experience. Of course, DuPre went on to do real grand opera. They did some things where he brought in very prominent singers to fill the roles and all later on. That was…there was no one in that except Furman Singers. I guess by some standards you might say it was not too professional, but we thought it was very professional and we loved it. It was a great time.

ROBERTSON: That seems to have been one of his focuses...

DENNIS: And also, we had, every Christmas, we had a big production of *The Messiah*. At one point he may have had 300 voices to sing. Everybody in Greenville who could sing and wanted to be in it was in it. It was beautiful music. It was standing room only in First Baptist Church, where it started, and out at McAlister. Truly, standing room only. A beautiful production.

That, coupled with the fact that he did something every spring, that pretty much filled the year for him. And also, I will tell you that he was the choir director at First Baptist Church for thirty-something years.

ROBERTSON: I've heard he led the rehearsals from the bass section.

DENNIS: Yes he did, and for church music, we had a paid quartet that sat on the back row of the choir loft. Each voice was pretty much responsible for leading the section. Only on special productions where we did bigger things...He would direct that, but when we first started singing *The Messiah*, we sang that at First Baptist Church. Of course I did all the soprano solos for a number of years. Mr. Rhame would do the bass solos. He would direct us all, and then when it came time for the bass solos, he would just turn around and sing those solos. It was an interesting time.

I was his soprano soloist at First Baptist Church for 27 years. I was married and had babies and continued to be his soprano soloists all those years.

ROBERTSON: Is there anything you'd like to add?

DENNIS: Furman Singers are an especially good group. I'm just hoping that it goes on forever. I know Hugh fairly well, and I've heard the Singers a number of times since he's been here. Of course Bing Vick is very close to me, almost as close as Mr. Rhame. I've sung with him. I've sung under his baton, and I have sung... When he first came, he and I did a lot of duets and trios and stuff together. He's been my friend ever since he's been here.

I've had a very special relationship with Mr. Rhame, and then 40 years with Bing, so you know that the Furman Singers are my first love as far as Furman is concerned.

Interview, Hugh Floyd, June 3, 2011

ROBERTSON: Could you talk for just a few minutes about your memories of Singers and Dr. Vick from your days as a student?

FLOYD: One of the things that I remember admiring about him a lot as a student...Bing, when I was there, won the meritorious teacher award my senior year. One of the things that was true then and has remained true was that it was really great as a student to know that your teacher was working as hard as you were. I found that really inspiring. During those years, particularly, he was watching himself on videotape. He was videotaping rehearsals and had gotten a grant to do that and was working on his stick technique and his rehearsal technique based on those videotapes. I thought that was really cool, as a student, in his conducting class, that he was doing that on his own with the major works, particularly the works with orchestra. I really admired him for that.

One of my happiest memories is watching him work like that. I also was a string bass player, so I got to double dip on the oratorios. I rehearsed them with the choir and then got to play them with the orchestra. The groups didn't conflict at that time. I got to watch him as an instrumentalist, too. It was really great for me because he was a model that you can do both orchestral and choral, that you don't have to choose. He was a big inspiration for me with that, and particularly with his relationship with Margaret Hillis, whom I then later studied with. That was really important in my life.

The other thing is the memory of being a student conductor. The work I got to do was the "Sanctus" from the *Mass in B Minor*. I don't know why he gave that to me, but to be 20 and to conduct the "Sanctus" with a choir of that quality was just an amazing experience. I remember, he was a really fine teacher about that. This was during the years of Joshua Rifkin. He had just come out with this idea of one-on-a-part, and frankly, that was the only *B Minor Mass* I had ever heard. I didn't know that it was done any other way. It was an LP that I found in what they used to call cutouts, in a cutout bin in one of the malls. When I was in high school that was the first and only recording I had ever heard. I was thinking Joshua Rifkin tempos and one-on-a-part, so you can imagine that it was different from what Bing would have done with Furman Singers. He was very polite about it…polite's not the right word. He was very supportive and brought me into his office to talk about Baroque style and it was just immensely helpful, and that helped it to all balance out into a more representative performance.

He was really great about student conductors—in fact, much better than I've been. He would meet with us at the beginning of the year, and we would mark all of our scores with his, which was really helpful because you got all of the repertoire and we sort of divvied it up. We did sectionals right away, so we had a lot of music to learn, but one of the first pieces we did that year was Schoenberg's "Friede auf Erden." Any man that can teach a 19- or 20-year old Bach and Schoenberg in the same semester deserves some credit.

It was an amazing experience. I can't tell you how hard that was, but I knew I was in a serious business. I didn't know until later how important that was. The repertoire of the Furman Singers was of the highest caliber. Three-fourth of the concerts was the heavy, standard fare, and then there was the lighter side. The great repertoire he did has stuck with me for my whole lifetime. Three years of that, the three years I was there, plus the oratorios—that's a real gift to somebody, especially since I learned both as a Singer and a string bass player.

Bing was a real scholar. He studied his scores and did his homework and set that as the bar: that you're expected to know your score and be organized and know how you're rehearsing. There was no flying by the seat of the pants. That's just not in his style. To get to be with a conductor…that your model as a student is a conductor who's that organized, and methodical, and prepared, has been a great gift through the years.

Bing was…his conducting is so minimalist, what he teaches, anyway. Minimum gesture for maximum result. I have to admit, I hated that at the time because I was a real physical, expressive, move all around conductor. But I was a good mimic, so I did it. I did exactly what he asked for. I've found that to be so helpful through the years to have a basis of conducting that's simple and small and minimal and clear. At the time, at 20, I didn't know that. I wanted to be expressive. I found that the ability to be small and technically correct was a wonderful thing. Once I saw conductors from other colleges who didn't have that same kind of approach, I realized how important that was.

The personal stuff is…from the very beginning of working with him, particularly once I was in his classes, which would have been the end of my sophomore year, I guess, I just felt immensely supported by the person as well as by the musician. I'm sure the other students felt that way too, and he was not a...I didn't get a sense that I was a favorite or anything, but I certainly got the sense that he would do anything I needed to help me get a job, to do the work I needed to do, to answer questions, those kinds of things. I felt, from the beginning, that he and Judy both have my best interests at heart. That's an amazing thing to feel from a professor.

I was spoiled. I didn't know until later that a lot of professors just have their next publication at heart. Bing really was about the students and immensely supportive of me.

I remember a conversation with him that surprised me at 20 but doesn't surprise me at 50. We were talking about grad schools and what I wanted to do and where I should go and what my goals were. I said, well, you know, what do you want to do? And he said, "I'm doing exactly what I want to do. I'm really happy here, and this is where I want to be." I remember feeling stunned at the time because the idea of, you know, being happy hadn't actually occurred to me. The idea that you could get a job that you liked and enjoy being there. I was so ambitious for the future. I was very...I won't say frustrated, but I was stunned by that. And now I'm in his office at the age of 50. I understand it much better.

ROBERTSON: Do you have any memories of tour you would like to share?

FLOYD: It's weird the things you remember. I remember him pointing to me once in a concert and making me fix my bowtie. I was embarrassed and also felt kind of flattered, like, he noticed that I was there. It was a fatherly moment. I think lots of people had that.

The idea of being on the bus tours, you know...everyone has their own stories about that. I was going through the files and realized how important where you sat was. I saw the signup sheets from when I was there, and it reminded me of the energy of worrying about who you were going to sit with and how tour would work. I saw all my friends and who they were sitting with, and all the relationship dynamics came back to me. I felt all the energy of wishing I had sat with someone else, or who I was sitting with compared to who was sitting over there. It just, it was very strange. It was funny to see, because mine was done in pencil, which meant that it was probably done at a later time and meant that I was indecisive. I was looking to see where my friends were, and people who I actually wanted to sit with, but you had to wait for them to sign up. It was very stressful.

We had amazing experiences on tour. We sang an entire concert of polychoral music for an ACDA convention in Tennessee. Double chorus things, and that was just really spectacular, a breathtaking experience, one I'll never forget. It was so much music for double choir, which, I mean, what kind of groups get to do that? That was a really rich experience.

I remember when I auditioned for Furman Singers student conductor, I did the "Battle Hymn," and I did "Ubi Caritas," the Duruflé. It went really well. It was just one of those days where things were in flow and it was really exciting and going well, until I got to the last measure of the Duruflé, and I got into that "amen." I got beautifully through the complication of that 5/8, got to the last chord, it was very, very soft, and I brought my hands down, and as soon as they were still they started to shake like nobody's business, like I had palsy. After what had been a gorgeous performance everyone just broke down laughing, so it was a funny experience. I still got the position, and actually Bing gave a rare compliment to me the next day in the conducting class.

You know, he seldom, at least then, called out a particular person to say that person did a really good job or this or that or the other. In class the next day they reported to me that he said that I had...they were talking about facial expression in conducting, and he said a good model of facial expression is Hugh Floyd. He said, yesterday he conducted the "Battle Hymn," which is our most hackneyed piece, and he made it into a religious experience. That sentence has kind of stuck with me all those years because I really had committed to the piece. His willingness to say that out loud gave me confidence and strength, even years later, in the sense, ok, I'm doing what I need to do.

I remember, in terms of tour stories, the lasagna every night. When we were there it was a lot of those big Stouffer's lasagna things, a lasagna tour. I still don't know the words to the blessing we sing... "The Lord's been good to me..." They just started singing that the first day and I've never learned it, still don't know it, we sang it on tour this year. I still can't get through more than a sentence or two. Now I just don't want to learn it. It's more fun not knowing it.

That time together was really important for what we became. Tony Stephenson and I, when we were in Florida somewhere, we were not supposed to leave the hotel and we went down the strip and got pictures made. So I'm really proud of myself. That was how naughty I was on tour one night, but I would have never...Now I'd kill my students if they did that.

ROBERTSON: Is there anything you would like to say about Dr. Vick's last year or the transition process?

FLOYD: Well, it's actually been very smooth and very wonderful. When I say that out loud, it sounds like I'm just pandering. But the fact is, Bing has balanced beautifully between helping when I need it and staying out of my hair when I don't need it. He's found a really good way of doing that. He reminds me every now and then of things to do, but has been really hands off in terms of letting me do stuff.

The students seem to have had an easy transition. They love him and miss him, but they're students. They know that things change, and they're excited about the new stuff too. Part of that has to do with Bing's officer structure. It is so intense, and it was so...I don't know how this transition would have worked without Cara Cavanaugh, particularly, who has a long family history with Furman Singers, and Rebecca Garrett, the vice president. Knowing what happened last year, the institutional memory that Bing sort of built in...You talk about keeping the same person all those years, and that kind of institutional memory really helps a choir. Fortunately, you know...kudos to me for not trying to reinvent it, and good for Bing for not saying, "No, you forgot to do it on Tuesday instead of on Wednesday."

He had gone through this, so I think he had a memory of what it is to be in the shadow of a well-loved and well-respected person. He built his own niche out of the DuPre Rhame era. They're very different people. No one thinks of them as the same, and that will be true for me and Bing as well. There'll always be love and respect, but we'll always be our own men.

I will say that the most exciting moment this year was riding the lift at the opening convocation. It was the first thing that I had done with the Furman Singers, and I remembered it so well. This was in McAlister, and coming up on that lift, we were all in the purple robes, and we had memorized our number, which had not been done in the past and could be really expressive. That feeling of rising up on the lift, which was a little hokey and very dramatic...I realized I was home and that was a great moment.

My favorite transition story is that, just the day before, Bing called me at the last minute and said, "Oh, you should check the switch. There are three switches on the stage, and if you push the wrong one, you'd only come halfway up and then have to wait and go back down."

Interview, Bruce Schoonmaker, June 4, 2011

ROBERTSON: You transferred to Furman from Davidson?

SCHOONMAKER: Right.

ROBERTSON: Could you talk a little bit about what it was like to be in Singers in those first few years?

SCHOONMAKER: Yeah, it was very exciting because he [Bing Vick] brought an energy and an intensity and a camaraderie that I had never experienced in a choral organization. Of course, he was espousing high demands, but he was always clear on how we could get there, and then when we didn't he wasn't just a jerk about it, when we got to those kinds of places. He had a maturity about him. I don't know whether he was working at it or whether I was just so young that I was impressed with it. He took what he was doing quite seriously, and that seemed to give a feeling of maturity about it.

ROBERTSON: Could you share any memories you have of the Christmas oratorio, tour, or the spring oratorio?

SCHOONMAKER: I remember the last opera Rhame did. I visited as an underclassman, and it was huge. They had this huge scenery, and apparently they had recruited fraternities to…you know, they didn't have elephants. They had lots of people. They also had some fairly big name soloists. They had two people coming in: Beverly Wolff [native of Atlanta, Georgia, 1928-2005] who had been at the Met, sang Amneris, and a younger singer, whom I can't remember, sang Aida. Jerry Langenkamp, who was on the faculty, sang the tenor lead. Carrie Daniels from Converse College sang the baritone lead.

It was a huge orchestra. I didn't look at the orchestra to see if it was all students or mostly students or professionals, but I would suspect it was a mixture. Rhame conducted it, and I think they did two or three performances. It was really big and overwhelming.

ROBERTSON: Once you came to Furman, do you have any outstanding memories of tour, or…

SCHOONMAKER: Well, one of the things that I wanted to add was that…a policy or a practice change when Bing came was that they nixed the big opera productions. They didn't have those any more. I'm not aware…I don't know exactly the reasons for that.

All I remember about the spring oratorio was a feeling of excitement and energy and a sense of accomplishment. I honestly don't have any specific memories. Tours, much more, a lot more memories. I'm trying to remember whether it was…We went to Chicago. I particularly remember feeling a real sense of accomplishment musically. I also remember when we were in Chicago we performed in the chapel at Northwestern University. I remember being very impressed by the organ and the music at the chapel. Not only the music that we did but also the music that the chapel choir and the organist and everybody did there.

Interview, Lloyd Linney, June 4, 2011

ROBERTSON: Could you talk a bit about being a Furman Singer in the last years of DuPre Rhame's tenure?

LINNEY: I entered Furman in the fall of 1966 and I specifically didn't want to be a music major, although everybody thought that I should be. I knew that I wanted to study voice, but I never had, and I knew that I wanted to sing in Furman Singers because I had heard about them. My brother graduated from Furman in 1965, and so I knew Furman pretty well. He was in the Furman Singers his freshman year but didn't stay in it after that.

We knew, my family knew about Mr. Rhame from a mutual friend, our minister's wife, in Washington, Georgia, when I went to high school. She had played piano in his studio and knew him quite well and wrote a letter to him about me, recommending that he take me as a voice student, which he did. That was my introduction to him.

I auditioned for him, and I can't remember if, at that time, I had to audition specifically to be in Singers. I know that, later on, you had to audition, but I joined Furman Singers in my freshman year and stayed in it for four years. I went on tour with them for four years and did all the other things that they did. I did study voice with him for four years, although I was not a music major.

ROBERTSON: So you took voice lessons from him. Did Mrs. Rhame play for you?

LINNEY: Mrs. Rhame didn't play for me all the time. There were a few semesters where he would have a student play for me, but many of the lessons that I had, many of the semesters that I studied with him, she was my pianist. I remember her as being very direct, sometimes intimidating woman, different in personality from him. I even have music where it has, in her handwriting…she would write "memorize" over on the side, you know. I was not a very dedicated voice student in those days and didn't practice a lot. I was a fairly good sightreader, and I remember standing, looking over her shoulder sometime when she was playing, and she would…I remember her saying, do you need glasses? And I said, I wear contact lenses.

I remember telling him many years later that I didn't practice very much, and he said, oh, I knew that. She was quite a little lady. And always very much a part of his life and a part of Singers, always went on tour with us. Short. He was kind of…he wasn't real tall, but he had a real strong character of body and she was just a short little lady beside him. He was a very warm person. He was kind of halfway in age between my grandfather and my own father, both of whom were very important in my life, and he kind of split that right in the middle. He was a fatherly image to me. I very much looked up to him, always wanted to please him. He was always very warm and very approachable.

One thing I remember about him is that he was always dressed very professionally, always had on a coat and tie at school. He wore a back brace. I'm not exactly sure what happened to his back, but he wore a back brace. When you would hug him you would feel that brace.

Maybe it was the end of my freshman year. I approached him because I did not have a music scholarship, and my father was wondering whether I could find some more scholarship aid. I approached Mr. Rhame and he said, "Well, I can't get that for you, but if you can sing in my choir at First Baptist, then you can get money for that." So I joined the choir at First Baptist that he also directed and sang there for my sophomore, junior, and senior years. That's how I met Carolyn Dennis. She was his soprano soloist. We sang two services on Sunday morning and one on Sunday night. The adult soloists, and there were four of them, would do the solos in the morning, almost always. At night he would give solos to various students, and I was also one of the sopranos he gave solos to.

ROBERTSON: Could you talk a bit about tour?

LINNEY: Tour was a definite thing. During the years I was there it was during Spring Break. We would leave on Sunday afternoon after the Sunday morning worship service. The rest of the student body left campus on Friday, and the Singers would be allowed to stay in the dorms on Friday and Saturday night. Some of us had church jobs at various places on Sunday morning, and then the tour bus would leave Sunday afternoon. There were always two buses. Mr. and Mrs. Rhame rode on one bus. Another woman…she worked in…she may have worked in the alumni office, she came with us and baked cookies. I remember those were always a big highlight on the tour.

By the time I was a junior, Jerry Langenkamp had become the assistant conductor for Singers. It was the plan that he would be groomed to take Mr. Rhame's place. He was a very outstanding tenor on the faculty. My freshman year he conducted Concert Choir and then he left my sophomore year to pursue his doctorate, I believe, or finish his doctorate. He came back my junior year. By that time Milburn Price had been hired to do Concert Choir. Jerry Langenkamp came back as Mr. Rhame's assistant, so he went with us on tour junior and senior years.

My freshman year our tour went to Washington, D.C. The picture I sent you was taken in Williamsburg because we stopped there to do some sightseeing. My sophomore year we went to Florida. We had one very long trip from Pensacola to St. Petersburg. We did not realize, I guess when Mr. Rhame was planning the tour he did the mileage wrong and he didn't know how far it was going to be. So it was a very, very long day trip and we had to sing a concert that night in St. Petersburg. I remember we weren't allowed to get off the bus except to go to the bathroom, and they sent the managers into McDonald's to get food for everybody and we had to eat on the bus.

My junior year we toured South Carolina, North Carolina…I guess that was about it. And then my senior year was the big tour when we went to New York City. We had a day when we were allowed to do sightseeing in New York City and go to plays and things, and we sang for the alumni association's New York Chapter. He wanted to do that as his big swan song.

The other thing that you may already know that he did as his swan song was a production of *Aida*. It was pretty outstanding, and I remember that I so wanted…Mr. Rhame used to bring in outside people or some faculty members to do the roles and students would understudy them with the orchestra. I had gotten to do that the previous year when we did *Elijah*. I got to sing the soprano understudy for that. When it came time to do *Aida*, I thought I was going to get to do that and I remember him saying to me, "You don't have an *Aida* voice," which is true. My voice is a lyrica coloratura. Another girl who was in Concert Choir got to do that understudy. We sang highlights of *Aida* on tour, and he let me sing the soprano parts then.

You know we did *Messiah* every year, and that was an especially meaningful thing for him, I think. He was not outspoken about his faith, but he would say things every once in a while where you knew that it really meant a lot to him, that the text was really important to him. He was that way about the anthems that we sang at First Baptist, too. I remember him talking that way about one of the anthems. It was an arrangement of the chorale "If thou but suffer God to guide thee," and it has been one of my favorites, too.

ROBERTSON: Langenkamp had a small group within Singers. Could you talk about how they formed and what they did?

LINNEY: That was, he called it the Chamber Singers, I guess. It was a small group that he basically selected. He asked me to be in that when he formed it. We would rehearse separately from Singers, but we were all members of Singers, and then on tour we would do a few numbers, just more like motets and things like that, Renaissance music, that kind of thing. One time I remember the Chamber Singers went down and sang a concert in Aiken without the Singers. I'm not really sure…there may have been as many as 16 in that group.

ROBERTSON: There was no continuity between that group and Dr. Vick's Chamber Singers ensemble?

LINNEY: No, I don't think there was.

ROBERTSON: Do you have any musical experiences that stand out to you?

LINNEY: I always loved doing *Messiah* with him. You may have heard that, when Bingham Vick came, he started doing it with a smaller group because he thought that was more historically correct. I remember Mr. Rhame saying to me at the first Singers reunion which was in 1979, when we all get to Heaven we're gonna talk to Handel, and he's going to agree with us that he wanted a large ensemble.

When we did *Messiah*, it was always Furman Singers and Concert Choir and then some people from town who wanted to do it. For instance, my brother kept coming back even when he wasn't a member of Furman Singers. The whole time he was at Furman he would always come back and sing in *Messiah* and even came back when I was a student after he had gone to medical school. That was just such a traditional thing. We would do it on a Sunday afternoon in the first weekend in December or something, and McAlister auditorium was always packed with people.

My freshman year the opera we did in the spring was *Il Trovatore*. I remember that I was not...I didn't think of myself as a fan of opera at all, but I was so surprised when we started rehearsing it because I realized that I knew all the melodies because my father had orchestral arrangements of the melodies. I thoroughly enjoyed singing in that chorus, too. In my sophomore year, instead of doing an opera he did *The Creation*, and then in my junior year he did *Elijah*, and then in my senior year he did *Aida* and that was the big thing he had always wanted to do.

Rehearsals were something I just wouldn't think of missing. I just loved being in Singers, and I loved rehearsing under him. He had such a way of drawing you in. I remember, I guess in my freshman year, we used to rehearse...of course we didn't have the building now. All we had was McAlister, and we used to rehearse two days a week over in the Townes lecture hall in the science building, and then one day a week we would rehearse on the stage of McAlister.

But I remember one of the rehearsals my freshman year when he was looking for sopranos who could sing high Cs for something. I didn't say anything because I was a freshman, and there was a guy behind me who had heard me sing in church choir back home. He said, "Lloyd, you can sing it," but I still didn't say anything. I remember going to Mr. Rhame in my next voice lesson and I said, somewhat timidly, "I can sing that high C if you want me to." He said, "Of course you can!"

I also remember my sophomore year, when he asked me to sing the solo…there was a medley of tunes from *Porgy and Bess* that has "Summertime" in it, and he asked me to sing "Summertime." When we got to the rehearsal, you know, he would skip over the solo, and then one time when we got to the solo he looked at me and he said, sing. I just started singing, and I had never done a solo in front of these people, and I remember people turning around and looking at me, like, who is this girl singing?

We used to have weekly chapel, and Furman Singers had to sing for chapel every Tuesday or Thursday, I can't remember which day it was. One year, maybe that same year, my sophomore year, he wanted me to do a solo of "O Holy Night." It was an arrangement of it, but it had a solo verse in it, and I think he didn't like the way I was doing it. I remember him walking up to me right before chapel started. We were already on the stage, and he said, sing it like "Summertime." I wasn't exactly sure how to do that at that point.

He had such a captivating way about him. He also had his own little funny things that he would say, just like I've learned many of Bing's since then. Mr. Rhame had a very fine voice himself. He was a bass, a really outstanding instrument. He would say, "Ok, I want to hear men and tenors." He would say that all the time. He would tell us how to dress correctly. He would tell the men to wear a four-in-hand tie, and I had never heard that expression before. He believed very strictly that women should not wear jewelry when we performed; we shouldn't wear anything in our hair.

ROBERTSON: Do you have any memories you would like to share that are specific to you?

LINNEY: I don't know if Jonathan's told you the story of his birth. You know he's named for Mr. Rhame. Jonathan's dad had met Mr. Rhame on several occasions. Mr. Rhame even recommended him for a position at Furman back in 1975, I think. Jonathan's dad was one of three people interviewed for that position. Jonathan's dad was very fond of Mr. Rhame too, so when I said, I'd like to give him Mr. Rhame's name as his middle name, he thought that was a good idea. So about the second day after Jonathan was born, I called Mr. Rhame from the hospital to tell him. I said, "We've just had a baby, and it's a little boy, and we've named him Jonathan Rhame." Mr. Rhame said, "For unto us a child is born, unto us a son is given." As soon as Jonathan was old enough to recognize the choruses from *Messiah*, I told him that story.

ROBERTSON: Could you talk a bit about the Singers reunions?

LINNEY: The first reunion was in 1979, when Mr. Rhame was still alive, and he called several of us that had been in Singers to ask us to be sure and come. I was actually pregnant with Jonathan then. I remember he called me and asked me to sing. He wanted to do the arrangement of the Schubert's "The Omnipotence." He asked Bob Blocker, who had been the pianist for Singers for a long time and had been there for two years with me…He was Singers accompanist three or four years and has been at various places: North Texas, maybe UCLA, he was at UNC Greensboro. We've always laughed about how many schools he's moved around to, but he's finally at Yale. Anyway, he asked Blocker to come back and play for him, and that was an extremely meaningful reunion because we had never done that, but it was also just a chance to be with him and also to get to know Bing.

That was in 1979. Mr. Rhame died in 1981, and so the next Singers reunion in the summer of '81 was one where we just talked and shared stories about Mr. Rhame and shed a great many tears. A lot of people had a lot of funny stories to tell. There's one story that Ty Talton told. He was dating Sandra Melton who he's married to now, and Ty and Sandra are the ones that did all the work to raise the money for the Bing professorship. Ty and Sandra were sitting near the back of the bus as were several other couples, and they told Mr. Rhame, "You should come back here with us." Mr. Rhame said something like…He was of course sitting with his wife, and he said something like, "Why would I want hamburger meat when I can have steak up here?"

My class, the class of 1970 was the one that spearheaded the Rhame Scholarship. Of course, over the years I've gotten to know Bing very well, and we've always had a good time talking because he teaches at my alma mater and I teach at his. He's invited me to sing solos at reunions over the years, and that's meant a lot to me.

I'm a big Furman Singers fan. It was one of the highlights of my time at Furman, and my brother, who has been president of the alumni association, told me that some of the most faithful givers to Furman are Furman Singers because, even if they don't have a lot of money, they've always been very, very loyal to Bing and Furman Singers.

APPENDIX B

BIBLIOGRAPHY

"A Brief Review of the Furman Glee Club – Day By Day." *The Furman Hornet,* April 15, 1922.

Announcement of a performance at the Piccadilly Hotel by the Furman Singers, undated. Furman Singers Archives, Furman University, Greenville, South Carolina.

Bainbridge, Judith T. *Academy and College: The History of the Woman's College of Furman University.* Macon, Georgia: Mercer University Press, 2001.

"Band and Glee Club Tour State Next Week." *The Furman Hornet,* February 7, 1936.

Blackwell, Gordon W. "A History of Brown Eyes." *Furman University.* Furman Singers Archives, Furman University, Greenville, South Carolina: 1981.

———. Letter to Furman Singers alumni, undated. Furman Singers Archives, Furman University, Greenville, South Carolina.

"Broome Elected Glee Club Head." *The Furman Hornet*, April 28, 1933.

"Calendar for the Week." *The Furman Hornet,* November 16, 1916.

Carmen. Concert Program. Furman Singers Archives. Greenville, South Carolina: 1963.

Cheatham, Patricia. "Rhame Will Conduct *Messiah* 29th Time," *The Greenville News,* December 5, 1964.

"Choral Club Has First Practice." *The Furman Hornet,* October 28, 1932.

"Combined Choir to Present Handel's *Messiah* Sunday at First Baptist." *The Furman Hornet,* December 4, 1953.

"Concert by A.C. Club." *The Furman Hornet,* May 2, 1919.

Cook, Harvey Tolliver. *Education in South Carolina Under Baptist Control.* Greenville, South Carolina: 1912.

———. *The Life Work of James Clement Furman.* Greenville, South Carolina: 1926.

Daniel, Robert Norman. *Furman University: A History.* Greenville, South Carolina: Hiott Press, 1951.

Dennis, Carolyn Whatley. Interview by the author, June 2, 2011, Greenville, South Carolina, Digital Recording.

"Editorial and Personal." *The Baptist Courier,* March 18, 1926.

"Epps Selected as Director of F.U. Glee Club." *The Furman Hornet,* October 8, 1928.

Elijah. Concert Program. Furman Singers Archives. Greenville, South Carolina: 1969.

Faust. Concert Program. Furman Singers Archives. Greenville, South Carolina: 1964.

Foy, Patricia S. "A Brief Look at the Community Song Movement." *Music Educators Journal* 76, no. 5 (Jan. 1990): 26-27.

"FU Singers Begin Tour January 26," *The Furman Hornet,* January 10, 1948.

Furman and G.F.C. Glee Clubs. Concert program. Furman University Special Collections and Archives. Greenville, South Carolina: Undated.

Furman Glee Club. Concert program. Furman University Special Collections and Archives. Greenville, South Carolina: 1924.

"First Glee Club Contest to Be Held Here." *The Furman Hornet,* April 23, 1923.

"Furman Glee Club and Purple Stringers Orchestra Give Delightful Entertainment." *The Furman Hornet,* April 22, 1922.

"Furman Glee Club Is Now Rehearsing 3 Times Per Week." *The Furman Hornet,* March 4, 1937.

"Furman Glee Club Will Begin Tour on Monday." *The Furman Hornet*, March 18, 1938.

"Furman Musicians to Leave on Trip." *The Furman Hornet*, February 13, 1925.

"Furman Singers, Band Begin Tours." *The Furman Hornet*, April 8, 1955.

"Furman Singers Rank Fifth in National Contest." *The Furman Hornet*. March 18, 1927.

"Furman Takes Second Place in Glee Club Contest." *The Furman Hornet*, April 30, 1923.

Furman University. *Bonhomie*. Greenville, South Carolina: 1901.

———. *Bonhomie*. Greenville, South Carolina: 1902.

———. *Bonhomie*. Greenville, South Carolina: 1903.

———. *Bonhomie*. Greenville, South Carolina: 1904.

———. *Bonhomie*. Greenville, South Carolina: 1905.

———. *Bonhomie*. Greenville, South Carolina: 1906.

———. *Bonhomie*. Greenville, South Carolina: 1907.

———. *Bonhomie*. Greenville, South Carolina: 1908.

———. *Bonhomie*. Greenville, South Carolina: 1909.

———. *Bonhomie.* Greenville, South Carolina: 1910.

———. *Bonhomie.* Greenville, South Carolina: 1911.

———. *Bonhomie.* Greenville, South Carolina: 1912.

———. *Bonhomie.* Greenville, South Carolina: 1913.

———. *Bonhomie.* Greenville, South Carolina: 1914.

———. *Bonhomie.* Greenville, South Carolina: 1915.

———. *Bonhomie.* Greenville, South Carolina: 1916.

———. *Bonhomie.* Greenville, South Carolina: 1917.

———. *Bonhomie.* Greenville, South Carolina: 1919.

———. *Bonhomie.* Greenville, South Carolina: 1920.

———. *Bonhomie.* Greenville, South Carolina: 1921.

———. *Bonhomie.* Greenville, South Carolina: 1922.

———. *Bonhomie.* Greenville, South Carolina: 1923.

———. *Bonhomie.* Greenville, South Carolina: 1924.

———. *Bonhomie.* Greenville, South Carolina: 1925.

———. *Bonhomie.* Greenville, South Carolina: 1926.

———. *Bonhomie*. Greenville, South Carolina: 1927.

———. *Bonhomie*. Greenville, South Carolina: 1928.

———. *Bonhomie*. Greenville, South Carolina: 1929.

———. *Bonhomie*. Greenville, South Carolina: 1930.

———. *Bonhomie*. Greenville, South Carolina: 1931.

———. *Bonhomie*. Greenville, South Carolina: 1932.

———. *Bonhomie*. Greenville, South Carolina: 1933.

———. *Bonhomie*. Greenville, South Carolina: 1934.

———. *Bonhomie*. Greenville, South Carolina: 1935.

———. *Bonhomie*. Greenville, South Carolina: 1936.

———. *Bonhomie*. Greenville, South Carolina: 1937.

———. *Bonhomie*. Greenville, South Carolina: 1938.

———. *Bonhomie*. Greenville, South Carolina: 1939.

———. *Bonhomie*. Greenville, South Carolina: 1940.

———. *Bonhomie*. Greenville, South Carolina: 1941.

———. *Bonhomie*. Greenville, South Carolina: 1943.

———. *Bonhomie.* Greenville, South Carolina: 1945.

———. *Bonhomie.* Greenville, South Carolina: 1946.

———. *Bonhomie.* Greenville, South Carolina: 1947.

———. *Bonhomie.* Greenville, South Carolina: 1948.

———. *Bonhomie.* Greenville, South Carolina: 1949.

———. *Bonhomie.* Greenville, South Carolina: 1960.

Furman University Glee Club. Concert program. Furman University Special Collections and Archives. Greenville, South Carolina: 1923.

Furman University Glee Club. Concert program. Furman University Special Collections and Archives. Greenville, South Carolina: 1927.

Furman University Glee Club. Concert program. Furman University Special Collections and Archives. Greenville, South Carolina: 1930.

Furman University Glee Club. Concert program. Furman University Special Collections and Archives. Greenville, South Carolina: 1931.

"Furman's 'Alma Mater' Will Be Thirty Years Old Next Tuesday." *The Furman Hornet,* April 15, 1937.

"G.W.C. Cantata a Success." *The Furman Hornet,* April 20, 1923.

George, Beth. "Female Leads Perform Well in Operetta," *The Furman Hornet*, March 12, 1960.

"Glee Club at Work." *The Furman Hornet*, February 14, 1919.

"Glee Club in Annual Concert." *The Furman Hornet*, April 15, 1927.

"Glee Club Is Heard By Liberty People." *The Furman Hornet*, February 6, 1925.

Howe, Sondra Weiland. "The NBC Music Appreciation Hour: Radio Broadcasts of Walter Damrosch, 1928-1942." *Journal of Research in Music Education* 51, No. 1 (Spring, 2003): 64-77.

"Glee Club Making Rapid Progress." *The Furman Hornet*, February 25, 1922.

"Glee Club May Tour European Countries Next." *The Furman Hornet*, October 29, 1928.

"Glee Club Will Render Program." *The Furman Hornet*, February 22, 1935.

H.M.S. Pinafore. Concert Program. Furman University Archives. Greenville, South Carolina: 1948.

"Harmony Hurricane Announces Tour Schedule." *The Furman Hornet*, March 16, 1934.

Herring, Gordon and Sarah. Interview by the author, May 9, 2011, Greenville, South Carolina, Digital Recording.

Huff, Archie Vernon. *Greenville: The History of the City and County in the South Carolina Piedmont.* Columbia, South Carolina: University of South Carolina Press, 1995.

Il trovatore. Concert Program. Furman Singers Archives. Greenville, South Carolina: 1967.

"Jimmie Taylor Is Selected as Club President." *The Furman Hornet,* May 1, 1928.

Johnson, David. "The 18th-Century Glee." *The Musical Times* 120, no. 1633 (March, 1979): 200-202.

La traviata. Concert Program. Furman Singers Archives. Greenville, South Carolina: 1965.

Linney, Lloyd. Phone interview by the author, June 4, 2011, Digital Recording.

"Local Glee Club Makes Tour Through North Carolina." *The Furman Hornet,* December 10, 1930.

Kegerreis, Richard I. "History of the High School a Cappella Choir." *Journal of Research in Music Education* 18, no. 4 (Winter, 1970): 319-329.

King, John M. *A History of South Carolina Baptists.* Columbia, South Carolina: The R. L. Bryan Company, 1964.

"Making Plans for Musical Contest." *The Furman Hornet,* April 16, 1925.

Martin, Agnes. "The Furman University Singers: A Brief History." Furman Singers Archives. Greenville, South Carolina: 1968.

McGlothlin, William Joseph. *Baptist Beginnings in Education: A History of Furman University.* Nashville, Tennessee: 1926.

"*Messiah* to Be Presented in McAlister." *The Furman Hornet,* December 3, 1960.

Mignon. Concert Program. Furman Singers Archives. Greenville, South Carolina: 1966.

M'lle Modiste. Concert Program. Furman Singers Archives. Greenville, South Carolina: 1960.

"*M'lle Modiste* Singers Operetta Production High School Weekend." *The Furman Hornet,* February 20, 1960.

"Motorcade to Hear Glee Club." *The Furman Hornet,* October 28, 1931.

"Musicians to Give Concert in Waterboro." *The Furman Hornet,* April 30, 1937.

Naughty Marietta. Concert program. Furman Singers Archives. Greenville, South Carolina: 1954.

Owens, Loulie Latimer. *Furman's Fairfield Days: 1837-1851.* Winnsboro, South Carolina, 1949.

Parker, David. *Discipline, Perfection, and Beauty: A History of Choral Music at Furman University and Greenville Woman's College, 1900-1987.* Greenville, South Carolina: A Press, 1988.

Pollock, Richard. Letter to the New York Area Chapter of the Furman University Alumni Association, undated. Furman Singers Archives, Furman University, Greenville, South Carolina.

"Progress Made in Practice of Play." *The Furman Hornet*, November 23, 1923.

"Purple Songsters to Defend Southern Glee Club Title Here Friday Night." *The Furman Hornet,* February 7, 1928.

"Purple Songsters Win Second Southern Contest." *The Furman Hornet,* February 14, 1928.

Regier, Bernard. "The Development of Choral Music in Higher Education." DMA diss., University of Southern California, 1963. In ProQuest Dissertations, and Theses, http://search.proquest.com/docview/302252354?accountid=4840 (accessed April 18, 2011).

Reid, Alfred Sandlin. *Furman University: Toward a New Identity.* Durham, North Carolina: Duke University Press, 1976.

Rhame, DuPre. Letter to the New York Area Chapter of the Furman University Alumni Association, February 18, 1970. Furman Singers Archives, Furman University, Greenville, South Carolina.

"Rhame Directs Operetta 13th Consecutive Year." *The Furman Hornet,* March 7, 1959.

"Rhame Selects Glee Club for 1930-1931 Session." *The Furman Hornet,* November 18, 1930.

Robin Hood. Concert program. Furman Singers Archives. Greenville, South Carolina: 1957.

Rogers, James A. *Richard Furman: Life and Legacy.* Macon, Georgia: Mercer University Press, 1985.

"Russell to Address Group; Furman Singers Perform." *The Furman Hornet,* January 8, 1954.

Sanders, Robert W. *An Early History of The Adelphian Literary Society University of Furman University.* Greenville, South Carolina: 1913.

Simmons, Beverly. " 'Brown Eyes' First Sung Years Ago," *The Furman Hornet,* October 17, 1959.

Sims, Rose V. "Operetta Lively, Colorful." *The Furman Hornet,* March 7, 1959.

"Singers End Tour Today; Show Here Termed Best." *The Furman Hornet,* February 7, 1948.

"Singers Perform for Kiwanis, S.C. Baptist Convention." *The Furman Hornet,* November 7, 1959.

"Southern Glee Club Contest Here Soon." *The Furman Hornet,* January 24, 1928.

The Bartered Bride. Concert program. Furman Singers Archives. Greenville, South Carolina: 1956.

The Creation. Concert Program. Furman Singers Archives. Greenville, South Carolina: 1968.

The Furman University Singers. Concert program. Furman Singers Archives. Greenville, South Carolina: Spring 1948.

The Furman University Singers. Concert program. Furman Singers Archives. Greenville, South Carolina: Spring 1949.

The Furman University Singers. Concert program. Furman Singers Archives. Greenville, South Carolina: Spring 1950.

The Furman University Singers. Concert program. Furman Singers Archives. Greenville, South Carolina: Spring 1951.

The Furman University Singers. Concert program. Furman Singers Archives. Greenville, South Carolina: Spring 1952.

The Furman University Singers. Concert program. Furman Singers Archives. Greenville, South Carolina: Spring 1953.

The Furman University Singers. Concert program. Furman Singers Archives. Greenville, South Carolina: Spring 1954.

The Furman University Singers. Concert program. Furman Singers Archives. Greenville, South Carolina: Spring 1955.

The Furman University Singers. Concert program. Furman Singers Archives. Greenville, South Carolina: Spring 1956.

The Furman University Singers. Concert program. Furman Singers Archives. Greenville, South Carolina: Spring 1957.

The Furman University Singers. Concert program. Furman Singers Archives. Greenville, South Carolina: Spring 1958.

The Furman University Singers. Concert program. Furman Singers Archives. Greenville, South Carolina: Spring 1959.

The Furman University Singers. Concert program. Furman Singers Archives. Greenville, South Carolina: Spring 1960.

The Furman University Singers. Concert program. Furman Singers Archives. Greenville, South Carolina: Spring 1961.

The Furman University Singers. Concert program. Furman Singers Archives. Greenville, South Carolina: Spring 1962.

The Furman University Singers. Concert program. Furman Singers Archives. Greenville, South Carolina: Spring 1963.

The Furman University Singers. Concert program. Furman Singers Archives. Greenville, South Carolina: Spring 1964.

The Furman University Singers. Concert program. Furman Singers Archives. Greenville, South Carolina: Spring 1965.

The Furman University Singers. Concert program. Furman Singers Archives. Greenville, South Carolina: Spring 1966.

The Furman University Singers. Concert program. Furman Singers Archives. Greenville, South Carolina: Spring 1967.

The Furman University Singers. Concert program. Furman Singers Archives. Greenville, South Carolina: Spring 1968.

The Furman University Singers. Concert program. Furman Singers Archives. Greenville, South Carolina: Spring 1969.

The Furman University Singers. Concert program. Furman Singers Archives. Greenville, South Carolina: Spring 1970.

The Furman University Singers. Concert program. Furman Singers Archives. Greenville, South Carolina: Spring 1971.

The Furman University Singers. Concert program. Furman Singers Archives. Greenville, South Carolina: Spring 1972.

The Furman University Singers. Concert program. Furman Singers Archives. Greenville, South Carolina: Spring 1973.

The Furman University Singers. Concert program. Furman Singers Archives. Greenville, South Carolina: Spring 1974.

The Furman University Singers. Concert program. Furman Singers Archives. Greenville, South Carolina: Spring 1975.

The Furman University Singers. Concert program. Furman Singers Archives. Greenville, South Carolina: Spring 1976.

The Furman University Singers. Concert program. Furman Singers Archives. Greenville, South Carolina: Spring 1977.

The Furman University Singers. Concert program. Furman Singers Archives. Greenville, South Carolina: Spring 1978.

The Furman University Singers. Concert program. Furman Singers Archives. Greenville, South Carolina: Spring 1979.

The Furman University Singers. Concert program. Furman Singers Archives. Greenville, South Carolina: Spring 1980.

The Furman University Singers. Concert program. Furman Singers Archives. Greenville, South Carolina: Spring 1981.

The Furman University Singers. Concert program. Furman Singers Archives. Greenville, South Carolina: Spring 1982.

The Furman University Singers. Concert program. Furman Singers Archives. Greenville, South Carolina: Spring 1983.

The Furman University Singers. Concert program. Furman Singers Archives. Greenville, South Carolina: Spring 1984.

The Furman University Singers. Concert program. Furman Singers Archives. Greenville, South Carolina: Spring 1985.

The Furman University Singers. Concert program. Furman Singers Archives. Greenville, South Carolina: Spring 1986.

The Furman University Singers. Concert program. Furman Singers Archives. Greenville, South Carolina: Spring 1987.

The Furman University Singers. Concert program. Furman Singers Archives. Greenville, South Carolina: Spring 1988.

The Furman University Singers. Concert program. Furman Singers Archives. Greenville, South Carolina: Spring 1989.

The Furman University Singers. Concert program. Furman Singers Archives. Greenville, South Carolina: Spring 1990.

The Furman University Singers. Concert program. Furman Singers Archives. Greenville, South Carolina: Spring 1991.

The Furman University Singers. Concert program. Furman Singers Archives. Greenville, South Carolina: Spring 1992.

The Furman University Singers. Concert program. Furman Singers Archives. Greenville, South Carolina: Spring 1993.

The Furman University Singers. Concert program. Furman Singers Archives. Greenville, South Carolina: Spring 1994.

The Furman University Singers. Concert program. Furman Singers Archives. Greenville, South Carolina: Spring 1995.

The Furman University Singers. Concert program. Furman Singers Archives. Greenville, South Carolina: Spring 1996.

The Furman University Singers. Concert program. Furman Singers Archives. Greenville, South Carolina: Spring 1997.

The Furman University Singers. Concert program. Furman Singers Archives. Greenville, South Carolina: Spring 1998.

The Furman University Singers. Concert program. Furman Singers Archives. Greenville, South Carolina: Spring 1999.

The Furman University Singers. Concert program. Furman Singers Archives. Greenville, South Carolina: Spring 2000.

The Furman University Singers. Concert program. Furman Singers Archives. Greenville, South Carolina: Spring 2001.

The Furman University Singers. Concert program. Furman Singers Archives. Greenville, South Carolina: Spring 2002.

The Furman University Singers. Concert program. Furman Singers Archives. Greenville, South Carolina: Spring 2003.

The Furman University Singers. Concert program. Furman Singers Archives. Greenville, South Carolina: Spring 2004.

The Furman University Singers. Concert program. Furman Singers Archives. Greenville, South Carolina: Spring 2005.

The Furman University Singers. Concert program. Furman Singers Archives. Greenville, South Carolina: Spring 2006.

The Furman University Singers. Concert program. Furman Singers Archives. Greenville, South Carolina: Spring 2007.

The Furman University Singers. Concert program. Furman Singers Archives. Greenville, South Carolina: Spring 2008.

The Furman University Singers. Concert program. Furman Singers Archives. Greenville, South Carolina: Spring 2009.

The Furman University Singers. Concert program. Furman Singers Archives. Greenville, South Carolina: Spring 2010.

The Gipsy Baron. Concert program. Furman Singers Archives. Greenville, South Carolina: 1958.

The Gondoliers. Concert program. Furman Singers Archives. Greenville, South Carolina: 1947.

The Messiah. Concert program. Furman Singers Archives. Greenville, South Carolina: 1956.

The Messiah. Concert program. Furman Singers Archives. Greenville, South Carolina: 1963.

The Messiah. Concert program. Furman Singers Archives. Greenville, South Carolina: 1967.

The Messiah.. Concert program. Furman Singers Archives. Greenville, South Carolina: 1968.

The Messiah. Concert program. Furman Singers Archives. Greenville, South Carolina: 1969.

The Mikado. Concert Program. Furman University Archives. Greenville, South Carolina: 1949.

The Three Musketeers. Concert program. Furman Singers Archives. Greenville, South Carolina: 1955.

"The Yale Glee Club: 1861-1961." *Music Educators Journal* 47, no. 6 (June-July, 1961): 81.

Thomas, A. "The Development of Male Glee Clubs in American Colleges and Universities." (diss., Columbia University). In ProQuest Dissertations and Theses, http://search.proquest.com/docview/302090972?accountid=4840 (accessed April 18, 2011).

Tollison, Courtney L. *Furman University.* Charleston, South Carolina: Arcadia Publishing, 2004.

Tomlinson, David. "Operetta Features Character Parts," *The Furman Hornet,* May 6, 1961.

———. "Character Parts Steal Show in Operetta," *The Furman Hornet,* May 20, 1961.

Tour itinerary, 1956. Furman Singers Archives, Furman University, Greenville, South Carolina.

"Tryouts to Be Held for F.U. Glee Club." *The Furman Hornet,* September 29, 1939.

Van Camp, Leonard. "The Rise of American Choral Music and the A Cappella 'Bandwagon.'" *Music Educators Journal* 67, No. 3 (Nov., 1980): 36-40.

Vick, Bingham, Jr. Email to the author, June 3, 2011.

———. Interview by the author, April 18, 2011, Greenville, South Carolina, Digital Recording.

———. Interview by the author, May 9, 2011, Greenville, South Carolina, Digital Recording.

———. Phone interview by the author, June 6, 2011, Digital Recording.

White, J. Perry and George N. Heller. "Entertainment, Enlightenment, and Service: A History and Description of Choral Music in Higher Education." *College Music Symposium* 23, no. 2 (Fall, 1983): 10-20.

APPENDIX C

LIST OF FIGURES

Figure 2.1 – The Florentine Bell Tower and surrounding campus, "Old Campus" location. Photo courtesy Furman University Special Collections and Archives. 16

Figure 3.1 – An early picture of members of the Furman Glee Club. Photo courtesy Furman University Special Collections and Archives. 21

Figure 3.2 – The Furman Glee Club of 1903. Photo courtesy Furman University Special Collections and Archives. 24

Figure 3.3 – A flyer for a Greenville Woman's College Glee Club concert, undated. Photo courtesy Furman University Special Collections and Archives. 27

Figure 3.4 – Furman students in field exercises, preparing for duty in World War I. The bell tower and old campus are in the background. Photo courtesy of Furman University Special Collections and Archives. 29

Figure 3.5 – DuPre Rhame as a senior at Furman University. Photo courtesy Furman University Special Collections and Archives. 30

Figure 3.6 – The front page of *The Hornet,* March 18, 1927. Photo courtesy Furman University Special Collections and Archives. 36

Figure 3.7 – This portrait of Nan Trammell Herring hangs in the lobby of the Nan Trammell Herring Music Pavilion. Photo courtesy Furman Singers Archives. 40

Figure 3.8 – DuPre Rhame. Photo courtesy Furman University Special Collections and Archives. 45

Figure 3.9 – DuPre Rhame and the Serenaders. Photo courtesy Furman University Special Collections and Archives. 50

Figure 4.1 – Furman University Singers and DuPre Rhame, 1948. Photo courtesy Furman Singers Archives. 54

Figure 4.2 – McAlister Auditorium 55

Figure 4.3 – From left to right, Jerry Langenkamp, DuPre Rhame, and Gayle Gulley on tour. Photo courtesy Furman Singers Archives. 60

Figure 4.4 – Mr. and Mrs. Rhame on tour in 1967. Photo courtesy Lloyd Linney. 63

Figure 4.5 – Rhame in rehearsal in McAlister Auditorium. Photo courtesy Furman Singers Archives. 66

Figure 4.6 – This portrait of DuPre Rhame hangs in the lobby of the Herring Music Pavilion. Photo courtesy Furman Singers Archives. 71

Figure 5.1 – Bingham Vick, Jr., in 1970. Photo courtesy Furman Singers Archives 75

Figure 5.2 – Grilling at the annual Furman Singers fall picnic. Photo courtesy Furman Singers Archives. 78

Figure 5.3 – The annual Furman Band versus Furman Singers softball game. Photo courtesy Furman Singers Archives. 80

Figure 5.4 – Vick's handwritten audition sheet for the 1980 fall audition. Photo courtesy Furman Singers Archives. 81

Figure 5.5 – Vick's signature and customary accompanying smiley face. Photo courtesy Furman Singers Archives. 82

Figure 5.6 – Furman Singers managers in the spring manager skit, a usual part of the spring banquet and naming of the new sophomore manager. Photo courtesy Furman Singers Archives. 85

Figure 5.7 – Vick in rehearsal in Townes Lecture Hall. Photo courtesy Furman Singers Archives. 88

Figure 5.8 – The exterior of the Nan Trammell Herring Music Pavilion. 91

Figure 5.9 – Peter Schickele in rehearsal with the Furman Symphony Orchestra. Photo courtesy Furman Singers Archives. 99

Figure 5.10 – Mosquitoes and Honeybees in concert. Photo courtesy Furman Singers Archives. 103

Figure 5.11 – Robert Shaw in rehearsal with Furman Singers and the Greenville Symphony Orchestra. Photo courtesy Furman Singers Archives. 114

Figure 5.12 – Furman Singers, Bingham Vick, Jr., and Keith Lockhart. Photo courtesy Furman Singers Archives. 118

Figure 5.13 – Furman Singers in the Cathedral of the Assumption. Photo courtesy Furman Singers Archives. 122

Figure 5.14 – A button given at the 1995 Furman Singers reunion. Buttons expressing loyalty to DuPre Rhame read "DuPre Directed Me." Photo courtesy Furman Singers Archives. 124

Figure 5.15 – This portrait of Vick hangs in the lobby of the Herring Pavilion. Photo courtesy Furman Singers Archives. 125

BIOGRAPHICAL SKETCH

Dr. Troy D. Robertson (b. 1978) is the Director of Choirs at Tarleton State University in Stephenville, Texas, where he conducts University Singers, Select Women's Ensemble, Texan Gentlemen, and Chamber Choir. Tarleton choirs are renowned for excellence: Tarleton's Chamber Choir recently performed in New York's Carnegie Hall and toured parts of Japan. Robertson is also the conductor of the Cross Timbers Civic Chorale, a community ensemble whose season regularly includes collaboration with the Fort Worth Symphony Orchestra. Performances under Dr. Robertson's direction have included G.F. Handel's *Messiah*, Johannes Brahms' *Requiem*, Francis Poulenc's *Gloria*, J.S. Bach's *Magnificat*, W.A. Mozart's *Requiem*, John Rutter's *Gloria* and *Magnificat*, Leonard Bernstein's *Chichester Psalms*, and Antonio Vivaldi's *Gloria*.

Dr. Robertson is an avid composer. His compositions include "In Meeting We Are Blessed," for SATB chorus and percussion, and "Love's Fool" for TTBB chorus and piano, part of the André Thomas Choral Series. The Florida State University Singers premiered his composition "This Mystery" under the direction of Kevin Fenton at the national convention of the American Choral Directors Association. Ensembles across the country have performed his works, which are published with Hinshaw Music and Colla Voce

Music. Robertson studied composition with Mark Kilstofte and André Thomas.

An active clinician and adjudicator, Dr. Robertson has served in festivals across the United States. Dr. Robertson was named a fellow of the Carnegie Hall Choral Institute's Transient Glory Symposium, an honor that included study with Francisco Nuñez, conductor of the Young People's Chorus of New York City, Grant Gershon, conductor of the Los Angeles Master Chorale, and John Corigliano, Grammy, Pulitzer, and Academy Award-winning composer. As part of the symposium Dr. Robertson conducted the Young People's Chorus in performance in Carnegie's Zankel Hall.

Before coming to Tarleton, Dr. Robertson was Assistant Professor of Music Education at Ithaca College in Ithaca, New York. He served for several years as choral director at East Gaston High School in Mount Holly, North Carolina. While at East Gaston, his choruses performed in festivals in North Carolina, earning a reputation for excellence and consistent superior ratings. Under his direction the choruses traveled to locations in Florida, Virginia, and New York's Carnegie Hall. Dr. Robertson taught alongside Trip McGill as co-conductor of the Gaston County Choral Ensemble. He also served as associate conductor of the Charlotte Oratorio Singers and Charlotte Chamber Singers under Scott Allen Jarrett, choral ensembles affiliated with the Charlotte Symphony Orchestra. In that capacity he assisted in the preparation of large and small-scale choral-orchestral works for conductors Christof Perick and Alan Yamamoto.

Dr. Robertson holds degrees from Florida State University (Ph.D.), the University of North Carolina at Greensboro (M.M.), and Furman University (B.M.Ed.). He is a lifetime member of ACDA and an active member of NCCO, TMEA, and TCDA. He is married to Dr. Stephanie Robertson, and the two of them make their home in Stephenville, Texas, with their son Winton.

www.ingramcontent.com/pod-product-compliance
Lightning Source LLC
Chambersburg PA
CBHW061253110426
42742CB00012BA/1902